182 Days in Iraq

Phil Kiver

Copyright © 2005 by Phil Kiver

All rights reserved. No part of this book may be used or reproduced
in any manner whatsoever without written permission of the author.

Printed in the United States of America.

ISBN: 1-59571-078-7
Library of Congress Control Number: 2005928825

Word Association Publishers
205 5th Avenue
Tarentum, PA 15084
www.wordassociation.com

Author's Biographical Information

Phil Kiver grew up in Cheney, a small town in Washington state. He graduated from Eastern Washington University with a degree in Political Science. After spending his college years in the National Guard, he joined the active army to participate in the current war on terror. With his new wife he moved to Fort Hood, Texas. While there he served as a broadcast journalist for the army and anchored a news show on NBC Waco. He also earned a master's degree in the History of the American Civil War. He was deployed to Iraq on July 18, 2004 in support of Operation Iraqi Freedom II.

Photo by Christina Vanyo

The author wearing his favorite Seattle Mariners baseball jersey with his cat, Nuisance.

Introduction:

This book is a firsthand account of time I spent in Iraq from 2004 to 2005. It is not pretty or heroic. What it is, though, is a personal look at what a soldier's existence is like on a daily basis in the War on Terror.

The actual title of this work is *182 Days in Iraq*, or however long the tour ends up being. But it ended up being one hundred and eighty-two days.

I am a broadcast journalist in the U.S. Army assigned to the III Corps Public Affairs Office, Fort Hood, Texas. In Iraq, I worked for the Multi National Corp Public Affairs Office, which oversaw media information for the entire theater of operations.

From the moment I boarded the plane for Iraq, I tried to keep a detailed, accurate, and current journal of my daily impressions activities and travels throughout Iraq. I wrote whenever the opportunity arose, using pen and paper.

This book is dedicated to those brave men and women from all countries in the Coalition who gave their lives in the hope of a more peaceful world.

18 July 1750 hrs

I'm sitting in an airplane on the runway at Fort Hood, Texas. This is a one-way flight to Iraq. I said goodbye to my wife about an hour ago, holding her close, only to see her turn and walk away. She didn't look back, only walked out the door with a sense of purpose, and was gone. It was the hardest thing I've ever had to do in my life. Our second wedding anniversary will be while I am gone. Shitty! We have two cats that live with us. One is middle-aged and wise. The wise one knows when I am leaving by the way I pack my things. When she sees that, she gets mad and hides. The younger one is just a kitten that doesn't know that my wife and I exist.

Well, the plane is revving up; I am on my way to war! What exactly does this mean? I am on my way to becoming a part of the War on Terror. Well not only a part but also a reporter and observer. Will I still have the same view when I return (hopefully) in six months or so? While I am behind the president and the army one-hundred percent, I can't help but feel a sense of—oh hell I don't know what it is but it's surely something different than I have ever felt before. But when have I ever been on my way to war? This is my first time so these are all virgin feelings even though they are in my heart and mind.

The army tries to make the last few hours easy and stress free at the gym where we depart from. There are video games, and free phones and Internet. They also provide a catered meal. There are boxes and boxes of odds and ends, such as socks and deodorant, just in case you need those last minute items. No one wants to sit next to a smelly guy on the plane. All of these things aside, it still didn't make leaving my wife any easier. I couldn't imagine leaving young children behind. I saw many soldiers hugging children or pregnant wives and girlfriends—hopefully, only pregnant wives, but that is a subject for another day. I miss my kitties.

1820 hrs

30,000 feet
I'm listening to a CD right now; music always soothes the savage beast in me. I always have listened to music whenever I could. Growing up I would have a stereo in every barn at my parents' farm. How different war is now than yesteryear—CDs, DVDs, phones. Many of my friends growing up were WWII veterans. They would wait a year during the war to get one letter. I sure hope it goes faster for me. I feel better now than I did before; it could be my medication kicking in. Alcohol is forbidden on this vacation to Iraq. Without giving away trade secrets, soldiers from the 4th Infantry Division gave me the low-down on how to operate. This is my version of "Survivor"; everyone is entitled to a luxury item, right? Of course, it could be that I am a liar, liar, pants on fire!

The in-flight movie has Meg Ryan in it. In two months I'm sure I will be glad to see anyone who isn't dressed as a soldier or an Arab. Fortunately, I have several laminated photos of my wife in my wallet. This will help greatly in the missing department. I know that wives and spouses' husbands don't get nearly enough credit for what they must go through.

The plane is now descending into Baltimore, Maryland. No one knows for sure if we will be able to get off the plane yet. It doesn't seem like it should be that important to get off the plane. However it would be nice to step on American soil once more if not the last time.

This time yesterday I was on my personal watercraft at the lake with my wife, far, far away from the reality of my situation now.

Several times I have asked myself, "How did I get here?" Like the verse from the eighties' song (I can't remember the name), "And I ask myself, what is the place? What a difference a day makes." I really love the sun and the water. I told my wife that when I return from Iraq, I want to go to Mexico for a solid month. Hopefully, while in Iraq, I will get a chance to swim in the Persian Gulf. Truth be told, I am very apprehensive about everything: Did I pack enough socks? Will my wife be able to sleep? What is my mom doing at home all alone while my father is away on business? Will my parents age more than they should while I am away at war? Is it fair to ask them to stay up and worry as all parents do.

Right now there are one hundred eighty-seven soldiers on this plane; we are all lost in our own thoughts. I like the volunteer aspect of the military. We all have that in common, although we come from different places. The soldier across the aisle is originally from Germany, the one on the other side is from Ohio, I am from Washington, and so on and so on with all the others on this flight.

2026 hrs

I'm laughing out loud because everyone on this plane has a rifle or a pistol with them!

19 July 1600 hrs

I am in Frankfurt, Germany, right now, waiting to get back on the plane from our two-hour layover. I was able to get ahold of my wife, which was very nice. It is 1000 hrs in Texas where she is. I don't think I'll take my watch off the time back home while I'm gone, that way I will always know what time it is there. I really think it will help keep my morale up. Last week at this time my wife and I were at the Major League Baseball All-Star game in Houston, Texas. I was working press for the army at the game. This was a real blast. I handed out American flag patches, like we wear on our uniforms, to players and fans alike. I introduced my wife to President George Herbert Walker Bush. He was very nice, taking a picture with us and signing some balls for me. He even kissed my wife on the cheek!

All of the soldiers on the flight with me were able to call home or use the Internet at the USO outlet here at the airport. I even logged on to check my retirement account and stocks.

Well, I am just waiting for the plane to take off for the flight to Kuwait. The cabin is very quiet right now, as all the soldiers seem to be alone with their thoughts. I tried to call my wife one more time before I got on the plane. She didn't answer, so I was freaking out, even though I realize she was just in the shower or something. But when you are thousands of miles from home, it is hard to be rational. The engines just started up, and the stewardess is talking about my seat cushion acting as a flotation device.

20 July 0001 hrs

I am in a bus at the Kuwait International Airport. My bus driver is an Arab, just like I have seen on the news. Honestly, his presence makes me uneasy. I feel like any minute he will blow himself and this bus up. I pulled out a baseball from my carry-on bag and started squeezing it very hard, wanting to be at a baseball game—anywhere but here. Right now I am hungry, exhausted, and more than a little scared. It is so hot here. When I got off the plane I couldn't breathe; it is like a blast furnace in this country.

Strange, no one is talking on this bus at all. I noticed a soldier sitting next to me just pulled out a pad and started writing, just as I am doing. I could really use a drink. I'll settle for a piece of gum.

A little about myself: I am the youngest of three; I have an older brother, an older sister, and then me. My parents are democrats, I am not. I will be voting for Bush again this year, they will not. My father is a geology professor at my alma mater, Eastern Washington University. I'm voting for Bush because I think he can handle the war on terror better than anyone else right now. I have met the president personally; I shook his hand and looked him in the eye. He may not be the best, but he's the best we've got. When I was at the All-Star game in Houston, I signed a lot of autographs because I am a soldier. After every signature I wrote 9-11. That is the date that will define my life, I'm sure.

0015 hrs

Still sitting in this dumb bus, no one seems to have any idea where we should be going. I am eight hours ahead of my wife in Texas, so I should still be able to call when I can find a phone. I don't want her to worry. But what can be done? The soldier next to me is from Houston; we had a short conversation about sports and junk—just nervous chitchat.

0023 hrs

Made it to a holding barn of some sort and caught a few hours sleep. Once the bus dropped us off, it was a circus. We got our body armor issued, then had to haul all of our gear down the road to this barn we are in now. For me, this was three full duffle bags and a huge backpack.

0900 hrs

I went to take a shower this morning, but there was no running water, so I had to use bottled. Imagine that: I yell at my wife at home for drinking bottled water; here in Kuwait I am showering with it. I'm just getting my body armor tightened up to fit me good and snug. In a little while we'll be flying into hell's kitchen and I want to be ready.

The heat outside is oppressive, as I said, even before you put all your gear on and haul your bags. The best way to describe it is that it would be like putting your oven on one hundred fifty degrees, crawling inside, and trying to do your daily business. I am listening to Toby Keith on my CD player right now. I met him and Willie Nelson at the Super Bowl last year. I wish we could all be friends with Jim Beam, but one out of three ain't bad. I won't call my wife again till I get settled in Iraq; it is 0430 hrs in Texas right now, and she needs her sleep. Once in the war zone, I may tell my loved ones less, so they won't worry. Well, fifteen minutes until we're supposed to roll out to the airfield.

1900 hrs

Finally made it aboard the C-130 that will be taking me to Baghdad. This is the road trip from hell. I feel like I've been hauling these bags all over the Middle East. We had to wait all afternoon in a shack on the flight line. It was very windy, with sand blowing so hard that it cut things. I'm putting on my vest and helmet now for takeoff. We heard a soldier was killed on this flight before. Some Iraqi shot at the plane and it hit the soldier in the back of the head. Crazy! Forty-five minutes till touchdown in Iraq. Talk to you soon....

2200 hrs

This is the day that I thought would never end. After we landed in Baghdad, we had to find all our bags in the dark. Um, I think mine is the green one; yes, I had three green duffle bags. Then we were piled on a bus, and I mean piled. Soldiers and bags going every which way. I was very uncomfortable; I had cramps in my legs and couldn't move at all. When we got to our camp, we all fell out of the bus, and had to find our bags in the dark—again. Yeah, I am still looking for three green duffle bags. What a circus! Finally, I made it to my tent. Now I am set up here on my cot, with all my worldly possessions around me. I even have a 110-volt electrical outlet, which is very nice. I think I'll plug in my DVD player and watch a movie. I know I should be tired, but with all these time zones I've crossed, my body does not know what to do.

21 July 1800 hrs

Just put live ammo in my weapon for the first time. I'm not one of these guys who gets an erection over looking at or handling weapons; however, I take my training seriously and can save my own life. So many soldiers, including some I work with, never thought they would end up in a war zone. I can't understand that mentality. I mean, it is the army, stupid.

Now I'm just trying to learn my way around this camp. Showers, food, shopping, mail, other units, and finding people I know. The most difficult thing is learning how the new office works. New people in, old people out. Politics, power plays, who's in charge of what. How much energy should I invest if I will only be here for six months? I just want to do my job, film some raids, and shoot some Arabs! Speaking of hatred for terrorists, it seems prevalent in my circle of influence here. "Nuke 'em, kill them, let us finish this war." These are all comments I have heard from other soldiers while sitting here writing. I can already tell some of these folks are full of shit liberals who don't want to be here at all. Specialist Birmingham is one of those who is against the war. She is a newspaper journalist from Fort Hood who I worked with before coming here. I simply can't work with anyone who is against what we all do.

I don't want to be hamstrung to the kinds of stories I can cover, although I'm sure it is coming. I just want to do what I can to support the war effort and have a good time doing it. I think I'll head to dinner in about ten minutes.

2100 hrs

Had dinner; lots of carbs, rice and beans, potato salad, gallons of water. It is so hot here, I have to drink constantly. I carry a "camelback," which allows me to have water on my back all the time. I'm constantly filling it up. I went for a walk around the manmade lake that surrounds the palace that is here in the camp. The sun was gorgeous, setting in the western sky. I've started making plans to get outside the wire and film some action. I need baptism by fire, just to get shot at once, and I will be okay. While I was on my walk, I was running in and out of the bushes, pointing my weapon at imaginary targets and dry firing my weapon.

22 Jul 0800 hrs

I skipped breakfast and came right up to the palace to check this place out. Right now I am sitting on the second floor veranda looking out over the moat toward the west, which is how you get to Fallujah from here. This is a spectacular view, but even here in the shade, with shorts and a t-shirt, it is unbearably hot. I called my in-laws and wife back in Washington State, but they didn't answer. She flew back to visit her family for a whole month, so that she won't get too lonely. Looking out past the perimeter fence this morning, I can see traffic and commerce happening on the highway. It is hard to imagine the level of violence that exists out there.

1100 hrs

Woke up at 0400 hrs, but I laid in bed till 0700, just trying to adjust my internal clock. I found my way to where I was supposed to be working. I met one soldier who works in my office. His name is Dubee. He seemed to be pretty outspoken, which I like; however, I really didn't like what he had to say. First, he said he was against public prayer. My response was that the Constitution clearly says, "Freedom of religion," not freedom from religion. Then he said he didn't believe in a hell. I told him when he gets there it will seem real enough. He made me so angry, I had to walk out of the office. Speaking of that, my office is a portable two-room trailer. It is set up in the backyard of Building Zero. To get to the trailer I have to walk in Building Zero, then out the back door to get to the yard where the trailer is located. I have only done it a couple of times, but it already seems like a pain in the ass.

Slowly trying to learn my way around. It will become all too clear and routine very quickly, I'm sure.

As for my other coworkers, most of them I know from my home station at Fort Hood. Great, I fly thousands of miles to see the same faces. I'll have to meet some new people quick, fast, and in a hurry.

I did get to talk to my wife today. It was a contentious conversation; she said I didn't appreciate everything she was going through while I seem to be having a great time over here. I sure hope these problems don't escalate.

2100 hrs

Just spoke to my parents on the phone for the first time since getting here. I managed to crack the code of how to call home completely free. It is sort of an urban myth; not many people know how to do it. But once you have learned, it is as good as gold in your pockets. It doesn't always work when you want it to, but what ever does? Here is the trick: you call any military base that is in the area code that you want. Once you get the operator on the line, you give her the number you want to call and she transfers you to that line—absolutely free. It takes a little longer than dialing direct, but it certainly is worth it. Will be flying out of here tomorrow afternoon to go cover a story up north of Baghdad. I cleaned and oiled my rifle, and grabbed 200 rounds of ammo. I certainly won't hesitate to shoot first and ask questions later. The world's worst trial is still better than the world's most beautiful funeral.

2230 hrs

I have taken my shower, shaved, and listened to artillery fire in the last few minutes. Nothing like hearing cannons fire while you are in the shower. Makes you want to stick your head out of the curtain and ask if everything is all right. The call to prayer for the Muslims has been sung as well. Our translator, who is Kurdish, told me that many times the call to prayer is really a call to arms. That said, I think it is only fair to meet them halfway.

I am very excited and nervous about my trip tomorrow. I am in the market to buy a couple of knives to shove in my boots. No one is going to take me prisoner! We have been talking about that a lot, with all of the beheadings we see on TV. Better to die fighting than be on TV with no head. Those fucking cowards with rags over their faces—God's will my ass. We have access to the entire collection of beheading videos here. Watching them is a great way to get to know the enemy and what they are capable of doing. Watching as they take over ten seconds to cut off someone's head puts it all in perspective. I feel they should show the videos on the news in their entirety so the whole world can see the savageness.

23 July 2200 hrs

I am at Camp Anaconda, fifty miles north of Baghdad. My wife's flight home was all screwed up; she had to fly through LA instead of Chicago. Here I am in Iraq, worried about her arriving home from her vacation all right. No, I'm not distracted. I came up here to do some interviews with a unit from my home state of Washington. I'll be spending the night here. Right now there is only one flight back to Camp Victory and it isn't until tomorrow. Well, I am… I don't know where this thought went to.

The trip up here was spectacular. Flying low and fast in a UH-60 Black Hawk helicopter, strapped in, widows open, camera in hand, with the hot wind in my face. It was awesome! Door gunners on both sides of the bird, but no shots fired—damn! The pilots keep us really low and really fast the whole time. Collectively, that keeps us really safe. What a great ride it was over Iraq!

Just came back from the movie theater they have at this base. *Shrek II* was playing; I didn't stay for it though; it was too crowded and hot in the movie theater. I did take a Nicole Kidman Poster off the wall though: *The Stepford Wives*. I am crazy about

Nicole. My wife never lets me forget it, either. For dinner I went to an outdoor picnic with the 29th Signal Battalion from Fort Lewis, Washington. The food was all from the mess hall, but at least we found a patch of grass and a picnic table. I did a story on their commander and shot some greetings home for them as well, which will be played in the Seattle television market.

My mission here today was a story about the 29th Signal Battalion; they have received literally tons of supplies from folks back home to give to the Iraqi locals. I interviewed the principal player, who was responsible for drumming up all the support.

While I was waiting to go to the movies, I had a conversation with a U.S. soldier who was against the war here, against the president, and it appeared also against me for supporting those things. He told me I was an angry middle-aged republican who had his head in the sand. He said it was the wrong war, and that Saddam really wasn't that bad of a guy to begin with. When he said that, I almost came unglued! Saddam gassed his own people and brutally oppressed anyone who dared to oppose him.

I'm glad the army takes all sorts of volunteers; that way it keeps things lively. This particular non-commissioned officer (NCO) was a large African American male. He kept moving closer to me during the conversation in an attempt to intimidate me with his size. I called bullshit on him and what he was doing. No one is going to intimidate me, especially not someone who was so stupid!

24 Jul 0612 hrs

I'm at the flight line now waiting on the helicopter to arrive. The air raid siren is going off because a few mortar rounds just came in. It's not like we can't hear the whistling and then hear and feel the explosion. Air raid siren—what do they think this is, the Battle of Britain? In Baghdad we just keep going about our business.

1145 hrs

My flight back was smooth flying. The door gunner fired his weapon into the riverbank just to make sure that it was working. Landed at the landing zone (LZ) and simply walked back to my office. What a way to travel. I'm coming to you now from the chow hall, where I am eating lunch. The food is all American style, with the caveat of being served by Hindus and Muslims brought in from India. I am having a tuna sandwich with a bowl of taco meat and pasta salad. I'm not going to finish it; I don't seem to be very hungry for some reason. I didn't eat breakfast either. My body is doing the same thing it did in basic training; I am using everything I eat and drink, producing little or no waste. I know it is kinda gross to talk about, but it gives you a lot of free time if you don't have to worry about going to the bathroom. Seriously, I haven't been to the bathroom since I got to Iraq.

25 Jul 0900 hrs

Good morning! One thing I don't miss right now is my cell phone. It is nice to be rid of it for awhile. I had a bullshit session with some random dudes in the dark outside the shower last night. Just a good ol' fat chewing session like you would have around the water cooler back in the states. My boss, Staff Sergeant Mann, is going off on Muslims right now. "It is just a pagan warrior religion!" I think this guy and I will get along nicely.

1630 hrs

Getting ready to blow the office and head to the swimming pool over at the Australian compound. After that I will be going to a pick-up rugby game the Australians have organized. They play every Sunday at the LZ. Since the LZ is pavement, the game will only be two-hand touch instead of tackle. When helicopters come in for a landing, we will all have to scatter.

I had some interesting inner office politics going on at work today. I think it is because I am so good looking and they are jealous. Maybe... or it is all the liberal fucks that pollute my space!

26 Jul 0750

I'm eating breakfast here at the mess hall with two captains I know from Fort Hood. They remarked how much like Denny's this place is, a real "get whatever you want to eat" kinda place. Alas, the more they make it like home, the more I end up missing it. Today I will film some hometown news stories for Fort Hood featuring the soldiers here and what they do on a daily basis. I slept very well last night, dreaming of home and happy memories from my childhood. I have been having these sorts of dreams every night, which is a great escape from the daily grind of being here in Iraq.

1700 hrs

I'm sitting in the sun at the palace pool. This is a pool where Saddam himself would swim whenever he was here. I once read an article in *TIME* magazine about how much Saddam would swim to stay in shape. This pool is very long and suitable for swimming laps. The changing rooms are huge, with gold fixtures and Italian marble floors. I was using the bathroom, thinking to myself, I am pissing in the same toilet that Saddam used when he stayed here. One interesting fact about this palace was that an Iraqi could be arrested for looking at it. It's true; when Saddam was in power, he personally selected those who worked in the air control tower at the airport. They all had to be loyalists, because they have a great view of what goes on over here. Amazing how this guy lived while his people suffered.

I received a coin today from the sergeant major for recruiting and retention. Army leaders give out coins for excellence. I received mine because he said I was good for morale. I also collected uniform flags from Australia and South Korea today. I am on a quest to collect something from every nation in the coalition. Yes, there really are soldiers here from other nations, regardless of what the news says.

It is so hot here that even getting out of the pool for a few minutes is unbearable. All the water does is make you wet, it doesn't make you cool.

27 Jul 1700 hrs

This has been an uneventful day. Well, I guess being alive counts for something. I have been editing some of my stories. I would like to fly out tomorrow, try to get back up to Camp Anaconda and stay away for two nights. I've gotta make some calls to catch a helicopter reservation.

All right, I just got the rez; my flight will be leaving tomorrow at 2000 hrs. My first night flight! Gotta go eat some dinner and pack for my mini-vacation. HA HA!

28 Jul 1000 hrs

I tried to sleep in this morning in preparation for my night travels. Unfortunately, the terrorists had other things in mind with their loud explosions outside the fence.

2007 hrs

Waiting at the LZ for my helicopter is getting to be a regular thing. I wonder if I should start applying for frequent flyer miles. In the morning I will be going out with a convoy to a local school near the base. This will be my first convoy on the roads of Iraq. Another journalist from my office is coming on this trip; that way we can look out for each other. He takes pictures while I watch for him, then he for me; that way neither one of us will be in unnecessary danger during the event. Right now I'm listening to the song "American Soldier" by Toby Keith. This song always makes my wife cry. She is on vacation somewhere in Canada with her brother's family. It's good for her to get away from the news. Well, it's getting too dark to write now.

29 Jul 1240 hrs

I'm here at Camp Anaconda again. Last night the helicopters were late arriving. Then we had mechanical problems with one helicopter. On top of the helicopters is this device that we call the disco ball. It detects a rocket attack on the helicopter, alerting the pilot to incoming fire. Well, one of them was broken, so it had to be replaced right there on the flight line. These Black Hawks that I fly on always go in multiples of two whenever they travel, so we had to wait for the second one to be repaired. When I arrived at the airfield here, we landed on the opposite side of where I needed to be dropped off. It gets so dark here at night. We caught the last bus to drive us to the other side of the base; however, the driver didn't understand any English. After driving around for about an hour, I told him to drop us off at the movie theater. This he understood; we were dropped off right in front. From the movie theater I knew how to get to the building where we were supposed to stay the night. I had the other journalist with me, plus we were heavy one lieutenant colonel that we had picked up. After walking for about ten minutes, we all made it to the 29th Signal Battalion. We spent the night sleeping on leather couches in the recreation room.

Now on to important things: my first convoy experience. We assembled all the vehicles and personnel in time to get our briefing from the convoy commander. The mission was to take school supplies to a school fairly close to the base. We saddled up and got ready to go. Rolling out of the gate I slapped a magazine of ammo into my M-16. My mind was set at ease hearing the sweet metallic snap of the bolt pushing a round into the chamber. There were five of us in the Humvee. The armor wasn't what I had expected; it was simply steel sheets that had been cut with a torch and attached in theater. The driver was a female, with all the rest being male soldiers. We started singing rock and roll songs to take our minds off the obvious danger of roadside bombs. Once we arrived at the school, the soldiers of the 29th set about off-loading the supplies and setting up different things in each room for the children to do. Once the children arrived, it was shear craziness: children pushing and shoving, with lots of crying; Iraqi men walking around with AK-47s, which is legal in this country, unless you are wearing uniforms of the enemy, which can vary from day to day. I can't really explain here how loud and confusing it was with everything that was going on. Some people were actually getting crushed in the humanity. I was running around filming everything I could. I stood by the door of the school watching children come out with armloads of loot.

They would run down the alleyway and stash it somewhere, returning just as quickly to gather more booty to take home. After we left, I'm sure it was like a barter fair between them. Some children even tried to sell the stuff back to us for money.

Once everything was gone it was time for us to return. I had to walk down an Iraqi street by myself, from the school to where my crew was pulling security. My other journalist watched me for those two hundred meters, as his vehicle was in the other direction. I never thought I would be walking down a street like this ever in my life. I was nervously scanning the rooftops, windows, doors, walls, and everything else. The locals were just watching me. I offered greetings in Arabic, my knowledge of which is limited right now. After what seemed like an eternity, I made it to my vehicle. I hopped in as the radio crackled out the rally point for the convoy to form up for the return drive back to the base. Iraqi children were following us on their bicycles, asking for American dollars in exchange for Iraqi dinars. We shooed them away, and picked up speed. With the convoy formed, we pulled out of the village and sped away through the Iraqi countryside. I was feeling better now, being on the way back to the base. Relief was complete when we reached the gate. First, we went through an Iraqi National Guard checkpoint, then the American point, and finally inside the secure area. Once we got back to the assembly area, we had an After Action Review. That is where you talk about what went good and bad with the mission and how to improve. One thing that I brought up was something that I had done. While strolling around the school taking pictures, I saw an Iraqi set his AK-47 down and then just leave the room. It caused me to become alarmed immediately. I picked it up, made sure the weapon was on safe, and held onto it until the soldier in charge of security came by; at that point, I handed it to him. It was really scary. In war, no one should just set a weapon down. The fact that he did made me believe that it was a setup of some sort, like maybe someone else was supposed to come pick it up, but then I intervened—who knows? Very scary! So I brought this up in the briefing, which was a good point. Everyone, regardless of their job, is a soldier first. Watch yourself, watch your buddy, and come home alive.

30 Jul 1830 hrs

Spent last night on the couch again in Anaconda. Flew out in the morning aboard Catfish Air. They are the National Guard unit out of Mississippi that handles the transportation assets up north. "Catfish Air: If you've got time to spare, fly Catfish Air." I wanted to purchase a unit patch with the fish on it and everything, but they were out. The commander had two thousand more on order though. I'm now in the chow hall back at Camp Victory. These air force guys at my table are talking about selling pet rocks from Iraq to make millions of dollars. Support the troops; buy a piece of Iraq.

31 Jul 2030 hrs

Only one exciting thing happened today. We were watching the secret computer feeds and saw some… well, we saw a terrorist get his; that is about all I can say about that. Right now it is one hundred twenty degrees, and I have the sniffles.

1 Aug 0900 hrs

I have a terrific head cold today. Just resting.

2 Aug 1400 hrs

This morning I had a very interesting mission. I went out to one of the gates with army lawyers from the Staff Judge Advocates office. Their task was to make cash payments to Iraqi nationals who had applied for compensation for acts committed during the war by American Forces. The payouts were for various things, such as a destroyed car, or crops, all the way up to children who had been accidentally killed. The total amounts ranged from a few hundred dollars to thousands. Army Captain Perry, who was in charge of the operation, spoke very well about how America has a system of laws and procedures in place for those who seek remedy under the American system of justice. It was rewarding to see deserving Iraqis get compensation; however, if destruction occurred through a legitimate act of war, no payment was given. If the loss took place through no fault of their own, or an accident, then they could seek and possibly get compensation. To get to these people, we had to walk past the American checkpoint to a low barricade out in the jungle. I was there with my camera trying to film, while making sure if a car bomber or shooter came, that I had an escape route planned. Running parallel to this road was an irrigation ditch, which I decided would be quick and easy to seek cover in if the spit hit the spam, so to speak. There were two young Iraqis who were giving me the eye and talking to each other while pointing at me. I leveled my weapon at them while with the selector switch on safe, just so they knew that I knew what they were up to. Right after I pointed my weapon at them, they got in their car and drove away. I don't think they came to get money; I think they were there to try to kidnap one of us. We had 1st Cavalry Division soldiers watching our ass, but that isn't much comfort when you are within arm's reach of Muslim men between the ages of eighteen and forty.

Well, everything went well with our mission today. I'm in my tent now, having lots to drink (juice, ha ha) and some cough medicine, which should put my lights out good.

3 Aug 1800 hrs

I put together a great news story today for the mission we did yesterday. I do all this great editing and production, but there is no guarantee that it gets played back in the states. No big surprise, this is good news from Iraq. The networks don't want a story unless it starts with "X number of American soldiers killed today in a roadside bomb." It's very frustrating sending these stories to my friends and family in the mail and having them say this isn't what we see on the news every night. That's an argument for another time. Now I am sitting at the Australian pool, as we call it. If it were not for the mortars, rockets, car bombs, and general mayhem, this would be a great vacation spot. The pool is located in the middle of the palace lake on an island accessible by bridge only. People play water volleyball or just get a suntan. The pool across the lake at the palace is closed right now. The only lifeguard went home on leave. Leave? What does she have to escape from? She works at the pool every day! At least I am out on the roads now and then.

The Aussies have a washer here by their pool; some young girl is putting her laundry in the washer right now. All of the guys at the pool look like there tongues are going to fall out. Well, when in a war zone, I guess.

For my next mission, I am going to the army hospital in the Green Zone to interview wounded soldiers and marines.

4 Aug 1700 hrs

Emailed my inquires to the appropriate folks today regarding my visit with the troops at the hospital. Hopefully will hear something back before the end of business today. A few minutes ago I was walking from one building to another when a mortar round came in and landed about four hundred meters away. Some Joe came busting out of the porta-shitter with his pants around his ankles. I can't blame him though; getting shelled in a shitter would be a fate worse than death itself. After seeing this, I think I'll head to my usual place at the pool.

I talk to my parents just about every day. They are against the president and this war like you wouldn't believe. My mother worries constantly, like any mother would, I suppose. I can hear it in her voice when I speak with her. My father worries as well, but I don't think he knows that I know. I listen to my CD player whenever I can. I know music triggers memories for most people, but I really use it to my advantage over here. My mind becomes a virtual scrapbook. It helps me to escape from the reality that I live in here. Some soldier across the pool just said my name. "Look at Kiver getting a suntan. What a metrosexual."

5 Aug 1300 hrs

New location today. I'm sitting in the front yard of Saddam's Tigris River palace. Well, it belongs to the Iraqi people now, not him. This palace is right on the river in the heart of the fortified Green Zone that you have heard lots about. I rode down here on a heavily armored bus, which we call "The Rhino." This thing is like a Winnebago on steroids. The windows are bulletproof with heavy steel all around. The driver, who goes by the nickname of "The General," told me it weighs twenty-six tons. We purchased three of them from Israel, but don't tell the Arab world that the Jews are helping out here, or all hell will break loose. Like it hasn't already. For the ride down I sat right in the front, looking out the window, taking pictures. Just like any other afternoon drive through a metropolitan area. Instead of playing *I spy*, we play guess which car is full of explosives. Right now the heat is explosive; I'm wearing all my gear plus weapon, camera, and tripod. I came down to do some recon at the hospital for my interviews. Since I'm here, I'm learning my way around the U.S. Embassy and Iraqi government grounds. Back in the states I like to film travel stories, to show soldiers where they can go to relax. This could turn out to be the same sort of thing. Hell, there are swimming pools and even restaurants here. I heard there was an outdoor shopping area, but I simply haven't had time to find it yet.

6 Aug 1030 hrs

Late last night was a goat rope, goose chase, cluster fuck… whatever you want to call it. Colonel Perry, who is the garrison commander back at Fort Hood, is retiring. The commander here, Lieutenant General Metz, wanted to send him a video message of congratulations or whatever. It was supposed to be sent by the 122nd MPAD broadcasters earlier, but apparently, something went wrong, so my bosses were freaking out like they lost the Zapruder film or some shit.

Someone needs to tell my command that there is a war going on here. There has been severe fighting over here in the last seventy-two hours; lots more than has been reported on the news. I don't have time to stress over a retirement video. Sorry, Colonel Perry, I like you, but I know you will understand.

7 Aug 1700 hrs

I am relaxing at the swimming pool. Well, more bullshit from Fort Hood contaminating the work environment here in Iraq. The short version is one of our computers back at Fort Hood was found to contain thirty-one thousand pornographic images, so the command is freaking out, trying to figure out who was responsible. My alibi is, well, I am in Iraq, you stupid fucks! They still asked me if I knew the password to the computer in question. Fucking retards. I told them that if they didn't find any images of Nicole Kidman on the computer, then rest assured, I am not responsible.

I am still dreaming of home every night. I pray that I won't have nightmares of this place when I return home. On the work front,

I did receive some positive email traffic about a story that I produced here; that made me feel good. I just had some girl take a photo of me with my disposable camera. My mom still wants regular photos for a scrapbook she is putting together. The girl who took the photo for me is not that pretty, but try telling that to all the dudes here at the pool. They want to talk to her, but appear to be too scared to do so. I have been here two plus weeks now. My morale is excellent. I still have medication, with more on the way. Made a couple of calls today to set up future missions, so life is pretty good for me here. The Shiite population is really getting in the attack mode right now; however, the Iraqi National Guard seems to be holding their own, or, as a British officer just said, "At least they are in the game now."

1730 hrs

Received a cool mission for tomorrow. Will be going out to the Baghdad International Airport to interview the Iraqi Olympic team before they leave for Greece. Saddam's son used to be in charge of the Olympic program. If athletes performed poorly, he would torture them, or kill their families. Yes, it is true; don't believe the liberal myth that the former Iraqi government was full of good people. The fact that Iraq is even fielding an Olympic team bodes well for the future of this country.

Well, the night is still young; perhaps I will catch the bus to Abilene. If you understand the reference, good for you.

One interesting thing I noticed today is how small the military community is: so many people have familiar faces, or they remember who you are from some other mission or exercise. There was lots of tough talk in the office today about just killing all these fucks, just like in the crusades. Don't fool yourself; the Muslims are out to destroy western civilization and all that live there.

8 Aug 2200 hrs

Well, I met the athletes today. What a historical moment. When we got out there, I just milled around the Baghdad International Airport like I was in Chicago or Memphis. I did some shopping at the gift store. I purchased some postcards. Then I went and had tea at a Kurdish run cantina. Never in my life would I have imagined that I would have ended up in this airport. It nearly blew my mind. The Kurds wouldn't let me pay for anything because I was an American. They said they really appreciated what the Americans had done for them as a people, so my money was no good to them. It was a wonderful gesture on their part. About the only visual difference between Baghdad's airport and one in the states were the security guards. They were patrolling the airport carrying heavy machine guns and side arms. Other than that, it had everything you would expect, including a duty-free store. Once the athletes arrived, they went through security, and then the gate. While waiting around, they seemed very shy and apprehensive about having their photos taken. Whenever I would move in for a shot, one of them would move in front of the camera—a rather effective passive-aggressive move. They had no issues talking to me through the interpreter or even listening to my ever-growing Arabic vocabulary.

Once everyone was cleared for travel, the team boarded a bus, which we followed over to the other side of the flight line. The transportation out of Iraq was being provided by the Australian Air Force. It is a shame that these competitors have to sneak out of their own country in fear of terrorists, but at least they are trying. There was a small ceremony involving the team and the ambassador from Australia. I was able to meet her, which was quite an honor. I have met presidents before, but this was my first ambassador. Watching the plane taxi down the runway and lift off into the sky, I felt like I had become a small part of what I hoped would be success for them in Greece.

Later in the evening I skipped a farewell party up in the palace put on by the "palace rangers," most of whom I wouldn't walk across the street to spit upon. As a punishment, I had to lay gravel in front of our work trailer. The Lord loves a workingman.

9 Aug 1300 hrs

I'm at the chow hall now eating lunch. They feed us very well here in Iraq. Here is what I had for lunch: one corndog, peas, carrots, plain tuna, macaroni salad, shredded mozzarella cheese, and pineapple juice.

1700 hrs

Took care of ho-hum errands today: laundry, cashed a check, cleaned my tent; but now I'm getting my afternoon sun at the pool. I just went kayaking on the moat that surrounds the palace. The Aussies have a huge kayak that you can use simply by asking. Kayaking on Saddam's former moat—what will I think of next? Tomorrow I will be going to the Green Zone for two nights and three days of "work." Lots of fun, doing interviews while getting mortars shot in my direction. I love it here! Take that, Michael Moore!

10 Aug 1400 hrs

I am in the Green Zone now. I rode the rhino bus down here again. I'm chilling at the pool behind the embassy with my feet hanging in the water. This pool is the best one I've seen in Iraq: two diving platforms, horseshoes, ping-pong, and a real lawn shaded by palm trees. Lots of different characters lounging about, too—diplomats, soldiers, contractors, you name it. I have been told that there were intense mortar attacks the last three nights. In fact, the tent I'm sleeping in has holes in the ceiling from shrapnel coming through. I almost forgot the best part; I saw an ice cold Miller Genuine Draft up close and personal upon my arrival here. Cool as a mountain stream. Too bad I'm not supposed to consume such nectar.

11 Aug 1200 hrs

Interviewed several wounded soldiers in the hospital this morning. They were horribly wounded, but had the best attitudes. They made me so proud to be a soldier in the same army as them. One young man was from Idaho, not far from where I grew up, yet we meet for the first time in a combat hospital in Iraq. Although these soldiers had wonderful things to say, I think I was more uncomfortable than they were. It was difficult to ask them things like, how's it going? when I see their destroyed bodies. I did my best to make everyone feel at ease. While these men were only a few of those hurt, I would like to think that all of them would show the same grace and dignity.

2300 hrs

This afternoon I was invited out to a gun range. Once out there, I received instructions on firing an AK-47. The teacher was a former Canadian army officer. The AK is an easy weapon to maintain and fire. It was incredibly hot at the range. While lying on the gravel, firing, the rocks were burning my skin through my shirtsleeves. Sweat was literally rolling down my face. It was like trying to work in a sauna. The conduct on this range was much different than how the American army runs one. We ran up and down the line, firing from different stances at multiple targets. All of the other students are private contractors who work as bodyguards for diplomats and the like. If it hadn't been so fucking hot, it would have been really fun.

I went out to a real bar that doubles as a Chinese restaurant with several new British friends that I had met this afternoon in the embassy. These men work as hired guns, protecting anyone who is willing to pay their fee. There were lots of other American soldiers at this bar/restaurant. I made sure there was always a glass of water in front of me, lest anyone think about turning state's evidence. Hard alcohol was available, but you had to purchase the whole bottle, not just one drink. So basically, it is a fifth, minimum. What a great country I am in right now.

12 Aug 1300 hrs

I spent all morning in the local shopping market here in the zone. The Americans refer to it as the bazaar. There are about three dozen stands and outdoor shops peddling just about anything you might want to purchase and send to your loved one. So I was just hanging out, talking with the vendors in English, Arabic, and Iraqi. There are many different dialects, just like in any language group. It was yet another experience that I thought would never occur to me. The Iraqis are very excited about their Olympic soccer team, which plays tonight. It is wonderful that, for once, they have something to be proud of on a national level.

13 Aug 0900 hrs

The Iraqi soccer team won last night. There was tons of celebratory gunfire throughout the city last night. For those who are not familiar with this practice, this is what happens.

Every swinging dick Muslim male grabs their AK-47 and walks outside; making sure their weapon is pointed in a safe direction.

There are two positions for this: either straight up, or toward the American base. Put weapon on full auto, gently squeeze trigger while yelling wildly about whatever your excuse is to shoot your weapon in the air. Also make sure to forget that what goes up comes down, especially if you are shooting straight up. Yes, I did mean to write it this way. In fact, I was outside my tent watching the fire when a round from an AK landed near enough to kick up gravel on me.

1400 hrs

I just finished shooting a story with the explosive ordinance demolition (EOD) soldiers. They have all these super high-speed robots that can spot and diffuse bombs, replacing the humans who would normally have to put themselves in harm's way. While the location and capabilities of these robots are closely held secrets here in Iraq, they are similar to robots bought off the shelf for police departments around America, so who are they really trying to fool?

Captain Kadlick, the company commander, invited me to go on a mission with him tomorrow, leaving at 1300 hrs, to Sadr City—very dangerous. I called and talked to my wife. I think I said too much; she was really worried about my safety.

14 Aug 1030 hrs

The convoy left early this morning due to a change in plans. They couldn't get a hold of me. I'm very mad I spent last night getting my mean face on. It was a huge emotional letdown, although if there is one thing I have learned here, it's don't question fate in a war zone—as long as you are still breathing, that is.

15 Aug 1630 hrs

The volleyball was missing at the pool today. Everyone was yelling, "Wilson! Wilson!"

If you get the joke, good for you. I was up very early this morning because of my noisy tent mates. I had a dream about my pet beagle named Lucy, from when I was a kid. She was a great dog, with no obedience skills, but lots of howling antics. I went in to the office to get some editing work done. Sergeant First Class Morrison, came down at 0900. She was in a pissy mood because all the officers yell at her, so she comes and yells at us. What a great organization. I gave her a list of supplies we needed for the office. She said, "Can't you just email it to me?" "I have it written right here, why would I email it to you? So you can print it out, or have to write it down again?" Some people are so fucking lost and detached from human interaction because of the fucking Internet.

16 Aug 2300 hrs

I'm listening to my Arabic language CDs in preparation for a mission tomorrow. I will be going out with a medical company from Ohio. They will set up a temporary clinic to treat the local population. This will give me a good chance to practice my new language skills. If there is a language that can save your life or mine right now, it is Arabic. Say terrorists take over your plane. If you can yell something in Arabic to distract them, however silly, they might not be expecting to hear that. Someone could jump them and save the day. Well, I hope it never comes to that, but I don't want to take chances. I didn't go swimming this afternoon. We had a planning meeting for the medical mission in the conference room at the palace. The officer giving the briefing is in the air force. She comes across like she thinks she is really pretty; however, she has a grill like a '57 Buick. Yeah, I said it; what are you going to do about it? The meeting time was a waste; I know how to operate out in the jungle. All she said was to pay attention to your surroundings and drink lots of water. No shit! Do I have a sign on my face that says *just fell off the turnip truck?*

17 Aug 2300 hrs

Had a very positive mission today. The medics I was with set up a temporary clinic in an abandoned building out past the airport. We had a difficult time initially convincing the local population to come and visit the clinic. They were afraid of retaliations from terrorists for visiting the Americans. Eventually, they treated one hundred two patients throughout the day, for various ailments. I also saw an Iraqi whose ten toes had been cut off in Abu Ghraib by Saddam's thugs. Guess you won't see that image on the nightly news, will you? It's a shame the real crimes go unnoticed. Of course, he didn't want to have his photo taken; I had to sneak it when he wasn't looking.

18 Aug 2300 hrs

Just got a brand new satellite uplink system today. It seems very complicated and difficult to put together. I may have to read the "destructions" (that is what my wife calls them when I try to put shit together). This system is used to beam out video or interviews live. It is sent to Atlanta via satellite; from there, any news station can hook into the feed. Pretty cool, and expensive. In a few days I'll know how to use it.

2300 hrs

Realized today that a change has occurred in me. I will explain more tomorrow when I have time.

19 Aug 1600 hrs

The change that I spoke of is that I am no longer afraid. I can now roll on convoys through the towns and villages without fear. I am doing things now that a few weeks ago I promised my wife I would not do. She refers to it as unnecessary risks. I call it doing my job, and having some fun doing it. Whatever, I am certainly a different person now than I was when I came here a few weeks ago. I assume (hope) that this is for the best all around. I don't want people to see that I have changed and be afraid of the person I have become. Birmingham said she is impressed that I always have a smile on my face and a song in my heart no matter what is happening around me. Too bad I don't care what she thinks about me.

20 Aug 0800 hrs

I came into the office and was working on stories this morning, when I realized no one else was coming in because it was Friday. On Fridays we don't have to come in until noon. So I shall go back to my tent.

1100 hrs Enter the Rat

When I walked in, one of my roommates, who works nights, was sitting cross-legged on his cot holding the broom in his fists. I said, "Hey, what's going on?" "There is a rat in here; it was crawling on my legs while I was asleep!" This guy is in the navy, and stationed in Corpus Christi, Texas. An okay sailor, but we are on schedules that are opposite, so we don't interact very much. I told him we should name the rat, feed it, thereby lulling it into a false sense of security, and then kill it! Savage rats in a savage land. Boy, they try to kill you every which way from here to Sunday here in Iraq.

21 Aug 1900 hrs

Rode in a convoy to a battered women's shelter at an undisclosed location today. The unit that I was with delivered a truckload of donated foods; however, what the program really needs is cash. They need money to pay the guards and improve the facilities. I met an army major from Civil Affairs who has been raising money specifically for this project. The Iraqi minister responsible has given her support publicly, but money has been very slow in coming from the government itself. Those working at the shelter hosted us for lunch. This was my first traditional sit-down meal in Iraq. It was grubbing good: rice, pita bread, dried fruits, stuffed ground beef things? Who knows, but it was all really delicious. These people can be very generous with what little they have, if given half a chance.

22 Aug 1450 hrs

The change that I spoke about a few days ago is complete after yesterday's convoy through the heart of the city. I feel invincible. The Iraqi soccer team won again last night. Please refer to lesson on celebratory fire, if you need a refresher course. I was almost hit again while standing outside watching the tracers cross the sky. You'd think I would know better by now.

Today is Sunday, so just about everyone gets some time off to go to church or relax.

23 Aug 1400 hrs

Well, the only news today is that my wife is returning from her vacation in Washington to our home in Texas. She has been traveling while I have been here in Iraq, on my vacation.

24 Aug 0815 hrs

I have Arabic classes today, although it appears the teacher is late. I thought I was going to be late; it has already been a busy morning. I was on the phone talking to my wife about bills and junk. Even with the phone and emails, it is still difficult to ensure accuracy from so far away.

Tonight I am leaving via helicopter to go back to Camp Anaconda. Tomorrow I will be on a convoy to check out the local electrical grid—something like that, not really sure. All I know is that I will be away from here for two nights, which will be like a dream vacation, without the swimming pool, but such is war, I guess. There was a massive explosion this morning, so loud that it woke me up. Usually I sleep right through those things. One guy moved out of my tent this morning. He is an army ranger who just reenlisted. He is going up north to Erbil; says he wants to do some killing. He has been stuck riding a desk in the palace for his whole tour so far.

25 Aug 0600 hrs

Had a good flight and a decent night's sleep. My escorts this morning are soldiers from the 1st Armor Division. A major, Chuck Larsen, is my point of contact here. He is a reservist from Iowa. He is also a state senator and chairman of the Republican Party in Iowa, serving proudly here in Iraq with the rest of us. What a great American. Our route is taking us past a known improvised explosive devices (IED) site. Major Larsen assured me everything will be all right. Love you, honey. Hope to see you real soon.

1930 hrs

Well, we are back inside the camp. Our Iraqi road trip lasted forever. We made at least a dozen stops to inspect different construction projects out in the countryside: schools, roads, electricity, water purification. All of these things are happening with Iraqi contractors and Iraqi labor, not Halliburton, like some would like you to believe. Iraqis are helping themselves.

2300 hrs

I managed to get a flight out in the evening rather than waiting for the morning rush hour. My flight this time was anything but peaceful. I was so tired from the day's convoy that all I wanted to do was sleep. The savages had something else in mind. Tonight's trip was on a CH-46 Chinook. These large two-prop jobs are big and slow. We were shot at the entire time. Bullets, rocket, rocket propelled grenades (RPGs), you name it. My tail gunner, boy, she was really firing back at them. The funny thing is, because I was so tired, it made me mad that I was getting shot at. Not afraid or scared, mad! I wanted them to stop so I could catch some zzz's on my commute. How fucking crazy is that? Speaking of crazy, my eye twitch is back.

26 Aug 1213 hrs

My wife isn't holding up well right now. She misses me terribly; I tell her she has it harder because here I have friends. In Texas she is all alone, with no family to support her, except for the cats, but they have no thumbs; how much help can they be? Meanwhile, her husband is always traveling, getting shot at, exposing himself to danger. She doesn't want me to remain in the army at this point. I want to stay so that I can get us moved up to Virginia for my next duty station. We would like to stay in that area and purchase a house. She likes Virginia/Maryland a lot. I was stationed at Fort Meade in Maryland for broadcasting school once. She came to visit and really loved the area. Since I like the Civil War so much, it would be a nice fit for both of us.

As for what is happening here, it is becoming difficult to juggle war/fighting, filming, professional development, Arabic classes, as well as a home life. My muscle spasms are now in both eyes, which is a great annoyance. I didn't realize what they were at first, but after talking to the doctor at the hospital in Baghdad, I understand what they mean. It is my body's stress reaction. They seem to come and go, but now they are intense. The doc assured me that they would go away when I return home, if not sooner. Going to the pool to swim helps, but only so much in reducing stress. I'm at the pool, but it is still Iraq. As for the level of danger here, I do feel untouchable. I have to have that attitude. I'm not going to sweat the small stuff. Like I told my wife, not everyone dies in war. Some always survive. I am a survivor. I'm the Sam

Watkins of the war on terror. Sam is one of my favorite soldiers from the Civil War. He fought for four years at just about every major battle, and lived to tell the tale. I even own his autobiography.

27 Aug 1400 hrs

Tried to head up north again today. No seats available on the regular Black Hawk flights. Did find a Chinook coming in at 2300 hrs that was going my way. Then Sergeant First Class Morrison said I couldn't leave because we are having a staff meeting in the morning. Great, my work is being inhibited so we can all have a meeting where they will tell us to do more work. Jesus, please help me not to kill those who are obviously so troublesome to me and to others.

28 Aug 1300 hrs

Am sitting in my tent getting medicated while eating pirate brownies. Arg! I am a pirate. Hee hee. I have a flight at 1500 hrs taking me up north. Right now I am sitting in my underwear—what a great visual that must be for others.

1930 hrs

Caught the helicopter, no problem. Four seats were taken by someone's duffle bags; looked like they were running away from home. In the morning I am on another convoy to see construction projects. One highlight is going to be visiting a veterinary clinic. Maybe I will get to see some animals. Now that I am here, settled in on a cot, I may go for a run. I'm spending some time in Senator Larson's office. He is super nice and very helpful in getting me around this area. The sun is setting, so it has cooled off to around a hundred degrees. Chilly—and me without my muff! Imagine thinking that a hundred degrees is cool. Since it is so chilly, I am going to go for a run around camp.

29 Aug 1700 hrs

Went on a road trip through the Iraqi countryside again. This time I was standing in the back of a Humvee with my camera on a monopod. For hundreds of kilometers, I stood with my camera in the wind. I didn't feel afraid, although I was in a vulnerable position. It seems crazy to go down roads where there have been roadside bombs. As for the reconstruction, I have seen it; it's nothing short of amazing when you see what they have accomplished in comparison to what they had when they started.

30 Aug 0700 hrs

Once again I find myself on a flight line waiting on a helicopter to take me home. When I say home, I mean Baghdad. Well, I was there waiting, then the bus came to take us to the flight line. We were dropped off by a helicopter. Then the bus came back, and the driver told us, "Wrong helicopter. No flights. Try again tomorrow." We piled back on the bus for the short drive back to the terminal operated by Catfish Air. I went right up to the counter and I said, "I need a seat, public affairs mission, priority one." They said, "Don't tell anyone; go, get on the bus." I did this; back to the flight line, on the helicopter, and home. Lesson learned: if you are not holding anything, it never hurts to bluff.

31 Aug 04 1600 hrs

Here at the pool again; first time in a week. I am beginning to suspect the mental state of myself and those around me. More on this later. Two young ladies of questionable orientation are here at the pool oiling each other. An older American here at the pool said, "That's the lesbo British girl with a new recruit." Needless to say, it was an exciting scene at the pool. This was exactly the type of relaxation that I needed after my traveling. Some of the regulars here asked me where I had been, commenting that they thought I may have been killed, since I wasn't at the pool.

1 Sept 1600 hrs

Today is payday. Not like it matters; all my bills are at home and I don't have a hot poker game or any obligations over here. Last night I had a horrible nightmare. I had a dream my roommate contaminated the tent with bugs. See, this tent mate in real life is a dirty man. He doesn't bathe, and when he removes his boots, it makes my eyes water. So I had this nightmare that bugs were crawling all over me. I got out of bed, grabbed my wallet, and headed to the twenty-four-hour mini-mart. I bought some razors, returned to the shower, and proceeded to shave my head. I also shaved my mustache and eyebrows. After I was done, I went back to sleep. When I got up in the morning, I had no idea what I had done. I was walking around and everyone was staring at me. I was like, what the fuck are you looking at? When Lieutenant Colonel Baggio saw me he asked, "What is your story?" I said, "You won't believe me, sir." He replied, "Give it your best shot." He didn't believe me!

One mortar round came in today, the first one in a few days; no damage. I was also electrocuted in the office today. I was messing with the wires under my desk when 220 volts blew me across the floor. Everything in this country is 220, so it requires converters. I could get a John Kerry Purple Heart for that.

Two guys here at the pool just asked me what I was writing. I told them it was a journal, so they started chiming in about things that they thought were interesting. Oh, wait, I just fell asleep listening to them.

I brought my DVD player to the pool this afternoon. I'm watching *The Breakfast Club*. Yes, it's old, but a very funny movie.

One thing that all of us in the office like to do is graffiti on the trailer next to ours. We do use dry erase markers, so it's not permanent. We only write the names of heavy metal bands from the 1980s. Now you can't just walk out and write whatever you want. It has to be inspired by conversation or song.

2 Sept 1612 hrs

I am at the pool for the third day in a row. Being able to tan and swim helps keep my morale up. Tomorrow I will be leaving to go down south for about a week, I guess. Will be good to get back out on the road. Here is an interesting fact: I have not seen a cloud in the sky since I arrived in Iraq. I just realized that sitting here at the swimming pool. I've heard the rainy season is coming, so I'll wait and see. I tried to catch a ride down to the Green Zone today; unfortunately, the bus was broken down.

Almost got a real kick in the teeth. Sergeant First Class Morrison wanted me to cover a change of command ceremony for the Italians. If this had been approved, I would miss my ride down south for the weeklong journey. In fact, she volunteered me for the mission before she figured out there was not a seat for me on the helicopter, plus Private First Class Dubee was already covering it for our office. Boy, oh boy, what will happen next?

3 Sept 2000 hrs

The flight down here was long and hot, with a full load of passengers on the Black Hawk. Flew east to Al Kut to drop some people off, then south to Nassaryia, and then west to Tallil, where

I am now. Saw lots of agriculture. These savages invented irrigation. The crops are planted in elevated rows; then the water flows between them where the roots can reach it. No need for electricity or such. Should be down here a week checking the progress of Highway One construction. This is the only road from the Persian Gulf to Turkey. Highway One... wasn't that the name of the main drag in Vietnam as well? Went to the ancient city of Ur today, here in Southern Iraq. Look it up on the Internet if you get a chance; it was very cool. Three different civilizations lived here in the past. There are also catacombs that you can explore and see examples of cuneiform writing that is seven thousand years old. These underground chambers were used as burial sites for the royalty throughout time. Because these people used a form of asphalt in their construction, the tombs have survived. The buildings are in remarkable shape. I also took a walk through Abraham's boyhood home, from the Old Testament. Three religions disagree on everything today, but Muslims, Jews, and Christians all agree that this is where Abe grew up. The entire area is covered with broken pots from the different peoples that resided here. I hope my digital photos can do it justice. The ziggurat itself is made from oven-fired bricks, with their own form of tar and reeds holding it together. This was definitely one highlight of my time here. Will be going back on Sunday to get a guided tour from the caretaker. His grandfather was part of Woolley's original discovery of the site back in the twenties.

The engineering officers I am rolling with are really funny. One is from the 420th Engineer Brigade, which is a reserve unit based in College Station, Texas. He (Colonel Bixler) turned and asked me if I was a bird watcher? I said, "Is this a joke? Are you going to say the word cock to me?" He merely wanted to point out that birds walk around with their mouths open to cool off. Well, I must be hot all the time as well. HA! HA! Colonel Bixler seems like a really great guy and a good officer. He is very short, but hasn't displayed any undesirable traits to me at all.

I had dinner in the Italian mess hall here on base: octopus, crawfish, chicken Parmesan—yummy, plus they served wine; I would like to go back when no one is there who knows me. Wink wink nudge nudge. It was like a mini-vacation to Italy in this mess hall. Everyone was speaking Italian, of course, and some of the food I just had to point at, because I didn't know what it was, and all these different languages are boggling my mind. I grabbed up a few cans of preserved food as well. I will send them home to my family for Christmas; maybe they can figure out what is in them.

4 Sept 0600 hrs

I'm going back out to the ruins of Ur this morning. We will be meeting the local guide out there in a couple of hours. I have done a bunch of online research about the site in the last couple of days, so I have the basics down.

Did I mention that this post sucks! There is no pool, no real bus system, and the chow hall is far away if you want American food. Yesterday I ate a breakfast burrito that made me feel really sick to my stomach. Yuck.

1700 hrs

The tour was very informative. I can't explain what it is like to be tramping through the ruins of what may be the world's first city in the history of mankind. I took so much video and still photos. Imagine being able to reach down and pick up pieces of pottery that are thousands of years old.

Had the afternoon off here at Talill Airbase, in Mesopotamia. I brought only the gear I needed with me, but luckily there is an Internet cafe where I can fool around on the computer. Will be crossing the Euphrates Highway River Bridge tomorrow, which will be neat. Just like when I drove over the Mississippi for the first time. The Iraqis are paving the entire stretch of Highway One, from Kuwait to Baghdad, which is very important for safety as well as economic development. The Americans provide the trucks and miscellaneous things, while the Iraqis execute the contracts that are paid by the government oil revenues. Work is slow but steady; sometimes they pave three hundred meters a day and others they do a full kilometer. There is roughly thirty-five kilometers left on the particular stretch to go. Will be going to the Babylonia city of Uruk (oo-ruk) this week as well. May even try to go out to the ziggurat tonight in the moonlight to see spooky things and generally scare the shit out of myself. But I'll see if that happens or not. Traveling here in Iraq, although free and fast, is a pain, and you can get hot quickly, having to lug too much gear around. Through trial and sometimes painful error, I have learned what is needed and how to get multiple uses out of the same items. For instance, clean clothes can be put inside of a t-shirt and used as a pillow, then exchanged for dirty ones, so that I have something for my head to rest on. I only travel with one little camouflage blanket, which is an issue item. The army calls it a poncho liner; I call it my tactical wobbie! Putting on a clean uniform to use as pajamas is one way of staying warm. The tents can get very cold at night with the AC running. By cold I mean below 75, which is freezing when you are used to a hundred twenty plus heat in the day. I bring disposable hygiene items that I just throw away on my way home to reduce weight.

When it comes to the gear, I always have my interceptor vest—about fifty pounds with accessories: helmet, weapon, camera, extra batteries for camera and microphones, monopod for camera, at least six hundred rounds of ammo on my vest, and water on my back, two gallons of which is for my daily consumption.

I carry two knives always, and may purchase a switchblade tonight that I saw a soldier with. It looked cool, plus it is one-handed action, which is key to survival. I carry a six-inch KBAR on my left leg. I call this my *I'm-not-going-to-be-taken-alive* knife. Designed only for killing, it carries a lot of weight when used properly; for close combat and, ultimately, prevention of me having to wear an orange jumpsuit. My second knife is a four-inch flip blade I carry in my right-hand pocket, used more for utility, but would slice a neck quick with enough force. Usually this is used for cutting rope, packages, bandages, etc. Other miscellaneous things I carry include a disposable camera, sunflowers seeds, pirate brownies vacuum-sealed from home, AA batteries, my wallet—you never know when you'll find an ATM—Chap Stick, notepad, two pens from Cheney Federal Credit Union, which is my bank back home, plus earplugs, sunglasses, sunscreen, pen flashlight, chemical illumination lights, and whatever else finds its way into my pockets. Needless to say, it is all very heavy and takes a long time to undress at night or empty my pockets for washing. Well, it is 1830 here; I think I will walk down to the Italian mess hall for some sort of pasta.

6 Sept 2300 hrs

Woke up ready to roll out onto Highway One. United States Army Engineers has been working hand in hand with the Iraqi contractors to pave the entire stretch, which has been without repair for at least thirty years in places. The pictures I took were typical of any highway project you would see in America: men laying asphalt, men making asphalt at a plant, and men leaning on shovels. Went and had lunch at the local ministry office to argue about the roads and who was going to pay for it. An exciting thing happened on the way into the compound. The driver turned sharply into a wall, ripping my M-16 out of my hands, nearly ripping my hand off with it. It wedged between the wall and the inside of the bulletproof door. I was afraid a round would go off in the barrel, causing it to explode in my face. The way the Humvee was configured, there was no way out; I was basically trapped. All I could think of was how embarrassing it would be to have a John Kerry Purple Heart. With some movement of the vehicle, I was able to unload the weapon, ensuring the safe removal of the round. Long story short, my rifle barrel was completely bent. At that point, I went from an army journalist to an imbedded reporter, armed only with three knives and my wits.

Lunch was served to us by the staff of the highway office, and was spectacular. We had a leg of lamb with rice, lamb sausage, beans, dates, soybeans, and Iraqi pita bread. Yummy! They fed twenty soldiers altogether. The lambs were freshly slaughtered, as refrigeration can sometimes be an issue in Iraq. After lunch, our convoy rolled out and headed to another ancient site to explore, but one vehicle got a flat tire. We pulled well off the highway to protect against attacks. We chose an area inside three berms of sand. The ground was covered with clamshells, and I realized we were standing where the Shiites of the marshes used to live. But Saddam had the marshes drained to kill the people and destroy their way of life. What a jerk-off. While changing the tire, we set up targets with cardboard boxes and fired up a lot of ammo. It was fun; I even fired the full auto heavy machine guns. Since my M-16 was busted, I fired someone else's M-4 rifle. I killed the box we were using as a target over and over, from about two hundred fifty meters away. Shooting is so easy once you learn. Free ammo and guns make the experience all the more enjoyable. As luck would have it, the spare didn't last, so we limped down the highway, which is lined more so with bandits than terrorists. We made it to a U.S. outpost and were able to pump up another tire. Thank goodness. But alas it was dark; our trip to Uruk will have to wait until tomorrow, after I interview some Iraqi highway patrolman.

On the home front, my wife lost one of our cats, which I found out by talking to her on the phone. She doesn't know how she got outside. The cat does have a computer chip from the Fort Hood Stray Clinic, so if she gets picked up, they will call my wife. I told my wife not to get upset, as it wouldn't help the situation. I adopted the kitty as a stray and am sorry she is gone, but I can't get worked up about it from here. Sometimes the war isn't as cool as it seems. I did learn how to say "I am dumb like a fox" in Arabic. What a funny thing to say to someone. I use that expression all the time at home.

7 Sept 2300 hrs

We drove the fuck all over MSR Tampa/Highway One, way up toward Baghdad. This road is a dangerous place—potholes, oncoming traffic, dust, bandits, but the construction goes on. The closer we got to Baghdad, the better the road became, with three lanes in each direction. We saw lots of herders bringing in the flocks as the sun went down. Camels just stroll across the highway—they are huge and not afraid of a vehicle in the least bit. When we returned, we saw tracer exchange on the Euphrates River Bridge between the Italians and whoever was out in the darkness. We killed the engines and lights, taking up positions around our vehicles. Flares went up: one from the Italians and one from us; my camera was rolling the whole time. We didn't feel like staying, so we hopped in and approached the Italian checkpoint. Just as we started moving I yelled, "This could be Blue on Blue," which is the army's way of saying *friendly fire*.

Sure enough, they fired at us with a 50-caliber machine gun. All we could do was jump out of the vehicle and run toward them. The funny thing is, had we been the bad guys, we would have taken the bridge from the Italians. This was my first experience with friendly fire. Birmingham was with me on this trip; she did nothing during the attack. She didn't take any photos or even react to fire like she should. Everywhere I look I see stupid people. After the Italians apologized, we hauled ass home, stopping only long enough to drop "Norm," our interpreter, off at the local police station.

8 Sept 0800 hrs

I woke up today very sick, with horrible stomach cramps and severe bathroom issues. Never felt like this in my whole life. I may have drunk bad water yesterday when some Iraqi construction workers gave me tea on the side of the road. At 2100 hrs, I called in to my hometown talk radio station. I was on for a whole hour with talk show host and ex-LAPD detective Mark Fuhrman. I was able to get a lot of the positive command message out and all the good things that are happening here in Iraq. It was an excellent opportunity to talk directly to the folks back home without going through the censorship of the news. I had to censor myself some, because he wanted to talk about causalities and the election, while I wanted to talk about building roads and power plants, and especially water purification, given my present state of bowel movements. Another great fact I got out was the number of other countries that have soldiers serving here in Iraq. Honestly, Mark didn't seem to have any idea that we had so many Allies helping us and the Iraqi people. After getting off the air, I was very excited about what I had accomplished and felt good about getting the information out about our troops and the jobs they do.

9 Sept 2300 hrs

Today was mainly waiting, and then traveling, just like back in the world. Go to the airport and then wait. I flew from Talill Airbase aboard a civilian C-12 turbo prop: leather seats, AC; two military pilots, no stewardess. Major Chisom and I were making jokes about that during the flight. I was cold, so I took off my top and used it as a blanket. I was still very cold. Then I heard Major Chisom snickering to himself. He had turned the AC on full and pointed it right at me. Jackass! While I was looking out the window, cruising at twenty-four thousand feet, for just a moment I thought, maybe I am not in Iraq. On our approach into Balad Airbase, the pilot told us to hold on. We came in very steep to avoid any sort of ground fire. It really felt as if we were falling out of the sky. We ended up bouncing on the runway. The flight was great though, a nice change from helicopter travel.

10 Sept 1500 hrs

Woke up this morning at Balad Airbase. I wanted to be in Baghdad. I crawled out of bed, found a phone, and called flight operations. I told them I needed seats for four personnel. They said to be there at 0730. Went back to the sleeping shack, turned on the lights, and said, "Get the fuck up!" By the way, I was waking up a major and a captain. "Get out of bed, we got a flight." They awoke slowly. I then went to the female shack to wake up Birmingham, the champion slowpoke. She said, "What is Major Chisom doing?" My reply, "He is getting his fucking clothes on; don't question me, I am a man of action!" Even with these other people in tow, I made it back to Baghdad. When traveling with other people, it is like carrying extra luggage that talks.

11 Sept 0900 hrs

We just had a large 9-11 ceremony in the palace rotunda here at Camp Victory. Seeing the images of that day over and over are very powerful. I despise people who say the conflict here has nothing to do with 9-11. Bullshit! The same fuckers who enjoyed that day are fighting us here. More come here to fight us every day, which is okay we me. Remember, in the war on terror, away games are preferred. You don't want to play defense at home like Israel has to do. While watching the video, I wanted so badly to cry, but I am a soldier, so I didn't. I'm sure I was feeling the same thing as everyone else in the room, though. The absolute rage that comes from that day consumes and fuels my hatred for the Muslim extremists. I have so much respect for those brave Americans who fought back aboard their flight over Pennsylvania.

We are wearing all of our protective gear around camp today: helmets, body armor, clean underwear. Hey, you never know. Just like Mom used to say, "Better safe than sorry"; that goes for the gear *and* the underwear.

2300 hrs

We didn't get shelled at all here today.

12 Sept 0545 hrs

Still September 11 in America. The bad guys launched nine to fifteen incoming rounds right over my tent this morning. I awoke to a whistling sound, which indicates mortars. They fly on inertia, so they spin through the air. Rockets, on the other hand, have onboard propellant, so they do not spin. So these mortars just flew over my tent. A new captain in my tent jumped up and said,

"We are under attack!" "No shit," I replied, "I read the papers." That is one of my favorite lines from *M.A.S.H!* So, this captain is freaking out. "We need to get under cover," he screamed. I said to him, "If you look carefully, you'll notice I am already under the covers!" I mean, what are you going to do if a mortar hits your tent? The bursting radius will ensure your destruction. I was afraid, to be sure; the mortars sounded just like they did in the movie *Saving Private Ryan*, when they are getting shelled on the beach. But hey, this isn't Hollywood, it's my life. As Bon Jovi would say, "I just want to live while I'm alive." Once the shelling stopped, I simply went back to sleep. How unconcerned I must appear to someone who hasn't been under fire. I was most disappointed that it was already the 12th of September—lazy terrorists.

13 Sept 1500 hrs

Just another manic Monday. I always try to listen to the song with that title every Monday. I have it on CD, so I try to remember to be manic every Monday, if I have the chance. Came in early to the office, at 0300 hrs. I had to show ID to Master Sergeant Battle just to get in the building I walk through every day on my way to work. When I got to the backyard where my trailer is, I noticed that the back gate was unlocked and wide open. How stupid is that? Watch the front gate and check ID cards while the back gate is wide open!

I went back to the front and told them what I had found. He wanted me to guard the gate myself. I told him, "We should go get the key together; I know where it is kept, and then we can lock the gate. Hmm, how about that idea?" I know I have a ton of college, but this isn't that hard to figure out. Sometimes it is a real burden walking around with your eyes open all the time while others are bumping into things.

I set my camera up on the roof of the building this morning to film incoming rockets, but the terrorists must have known I was waiting, so they did not attack. I was most disappointed.

14 Sept. 0130 hrs

Just when I thought things couldn't get any dumber, they kept the interior guards for another day. Since we have been getting shelled with mortars and rockets, they've posted guards throughout camp. What good is that going to do? Are the guards going to shoot the rockets down? Or maybe ask them to show some form of ID? What do I know; I'm not in charge. It just seems stupid. If we had problems with infiltrators, I could see taking these precautions, but really. Talk about a knee-jerk reaction. How about we send patrols out to kill the fuckers who are shelling us?

I'm getting close to my (alleged) half-way point of my tour. Should be going home sometime in January. Home ... what will that be like for me now? I certainly won't jump at loud noises anymore. I tell myself things will be okay, but I'm not so sure. My tolerance for violence and mayhem has grown. I'll be at a Yankees game in New York and see some dude get stabbed and say to him, "That's not so bad." The change in me has been enormous. I see it now, and have spoken about it before. I am frightened that my loved ones may find it alarming when I return home. I can look at bodies burning because of a car bomb and just calmly take the picture. I know that means I am a professional, but have I lost some of my humanity in the process? My answer is yes, I have, but will that make me less sensitive to the suffering of others? I don't want to be one of those crazy veterans on the street. One thing I'll surely have a problem with is sleeping without helicopters flying over my tent at all hours.

Our cats have become like people to my wife and me. They keep my wife company when she is home. She even puts them on the phone so I can talk to them, or she'll have me yell at them if they have been bad. Is that crazy? We don't have any children right now. For that I am thankful. That sounds dumb, being thankful for not having a family. "Where's Daddy?" He went to the store and will be back in six months. Fuck that!

On the work front, the 420th Engineers wanted me to brief their commander, Brigadier General Pullhman, about the stories I have covered for them here in Iraq. My boss, Lt. Col. Dan Baggio, said that I was not seasoned enough to give a briefing to a general. Further, he wanted me to give my briefing to him, so then he, in turn, could brief the general. That didn't seem fair to me at all. Nor does it make much sense. The general wants to hear what I have to say, not a watered down version.

15 Sept. 1440 hrs

Chilling outside my tent. I have a meeting with Colonel Pannitzi of the Italian Army at 1600 hrs. Today, while I was filming a meeting of all the foreign commanders, this colonel invited me to travel with the Italians and film their trip to Nassaryia for lunch on Sunday. Even though they want me to film, it is quite an honor. I had been told that only Italians could eat in their mess hall on Sundays because of some tradition. Of course, it is over an hour by helicopter to fly there. One soldier in my office said that would be like flying to London for a haircut. I sometimes wonder if I am having a "one of a kind" experience here in Iraq, or do other soldiers get to do fun things like this? I call home a lot. I usually call friends from my hometown that I haven't spoken to in a while just to let them know how I am doing and that I have not forgotten about them. A few days ago I called the mother of a boy I went to school with all the way through to graduation. Robin was happy to hear I was doing well over here.

She said, "We always knew you needed some excitement in your life." She didn't know that I was over here until my sister told her. They both teach at my hometown middle school in Cheney, Washington. It was nice talking to her; she said that she'd be praying for me.

My eye twitch is back. It is the stress of being here around the palace, getting shelled—combined with the people I work with. It is all the hassle of "hanging around the flagpole," as the expression goes.

16 Sept 1800 hrs

Sergeant, First Class Nancy Morrison is being a total wretch to me, for who knows what reasons. Oh, she tells me what she thinks, but I can't help that I don't believe her at all. Tonight at 2000 hrs, we have to put all our protective gear on, as the army is engaged in offensive operations in the Sunni Triangle. So the Intel guys think we will be attacked. That said, we have to walk around in our turtle gear. Right now I am going to take a nap and head in to the office later to get some night work done. Hopefully, I'll have some mail from home waiting for me on my desk.

17 Sept 2200 hrs

Had a going away party tonight for someone I actually knew. There is an imbedded Fox News reporter hanging out for the next three days or so. Last year he was a battalion commander in the 3rd Infantry Division. He was engaged in the "Thunder Run" that drove through the heart of Baghdad. He is a good resource to talk to; however, I am still against civilian reporters being here. I just think they do more harm than good. I am an army reporter, so just let me do my job without having to worry about where I am and what I'm doing, like we do with civilian reporters.

18 Sept 2200 hrs

Went to the rifle range today to fire my M-16. The range here is to those standards that we would train on in the United States. The target is twenty-five meters away, with different size silhouettes to simulate varying distances. It was so very hot out there. Sweat kept rolling down my face into my eyes. I hit thirty out of forty, which is about average for me; however, this was the first time I had to fire under range conditions with my body armor on. After that round of qualifying, I had to shoot with my gas mask on. This time I hit sixteen out of twenty, which was really good. After that, we came back out for night fire. It is still the same distance, but now it is pitch black. They give us tracer rounds, which illuminate as they fly through the air, thus showing us where the target is for the next round.

On to other things; Baghdad seems to be turning into a very dangerous place. Today was the first time I had that thought; however, the countryside that I have traveled through seems to be settling down very nicely. But in the city there are always massive explosions. In fact, I just heard one.

It seems terrorist leaders are paying young men two hundred dollars to become suicide car bombers, promising them they will go to heaven to be with lots of virgin maidens. Oh, if only it were that easy. Plus, I know I have done my share to ensure that there are no redheaded virgins left for those assholes.

19 Sept 2300 hrs

Today was one of my best and most enjoyable days so far in Iraq. Well, I have had lots of fun at the pool, a time or three. My wife teaches me these tricky phrases. Anyhow, I went to the LZ at 0715 to catch a ride with the Italians who wanted my video support. I sure enjoy traveling by helicopter, until mine gets shots down. Hopefully, that will never happen. Well, we flew south for an hour and a half, landing at Talill Airbase, where I had been working only a couple of weeks ago. I was there to accompany the senior Italian leader in Iraq. After we landed, we waited for the Italian Chairman of the Joint Chiefs of Staff. His arrival had been a closely guarded secret because of his position and status. Although I have waited on lots of flight lines, this was a lot better. I was able to swap unit patches and practice my limited Italian. Once the chairman arrived, we went to our initial briefing on the situation in this part of Iraq, where the Italian forces have control. Then we began a whirlwind helicopter tour, landing at the same Euphrates River Bridge where I had been shot at before.

This trip was lots of fun because I was aboard Italian helicopters. They got us where we needed to be, but it was a different experience. I'm sure they feel the same way riding in American helicopters. After the bridge, we landed at the base and hopped into an armored convoy for a trip through the heart of Nassaryia. The Italians really showed me something in their convoy tactics: driving all over the road, two wide, three wide, single file; it was a blast, yet I felt safe the entire time. I was able to stand up and put my upper body outside the hatch so I could film the street action. The vans we were using reminded me of the old black van the A-Team used to drive on their TV show.

I saw some of Mutata Al-Sadr's recruiting stands along the roadside in the city. You can tell by the green and black banners they fly. One thing that I had never seen before was billboards of the influential religious leaders all along the road. I had seen them on TV, but it was much more powerful to see in person. There is no such thing as separation of church and state here in Iraq, and probably the Middle East as a whole. After the road trip, it was back to the Italian camp for another briefing. I actually fell asleep during this one, but what the hell, I don't understand Italian at all. Well, a little, but surely not enough to pay attention during a military briefing. I did see a general who carried a riding whip around behind his back; I took many pictures of him. After the meeting, the party wanted to go out to the ziggurat again. Everyone who visits this part of Iraq goes out there, which is fine with me. I had received a mission to interview the tour guide again. For reasons which I can't reveal in this book, it had to be in Arabic, and there were key phrases that I wanted him to say. It all went according to plan, which was a good thing for everyone involved.

2200 hrs

After our tour, it was dinnertime in the Italian mess hall. Tonight I had roast beef with tomatoes and Swiss cheese covered in a heavenly lemon sauce. What a decadent treat. I topped it off with Parmesan cheese, not the grated stuff we Americans swill—whole chunks that I had to eat with my hand. How absolutely continental. After dinner, my guide, an Italian major, enlisted soldiers, and I went bar hopping through the Italian camp. Since I am not allowed to drink, I surely didn't have two amarettos. I never know when the spies are out.

20 Sept 1000 hrs

Will be leaving this area of operations at 1200 hrs aboard another Black Hawk. One good Italian I have met here is 1st Lt. Roberto Furlani. A great guy, although he stands very close to me, which is a European thing. I need my space. I grew up out West, with a driveway that was a mile long. He speaks perfect English, and was once an exchange student in the Seattle area. He agreed to be on the radio with me when I do a live broadcast back to the Seattle market. This should be very beneficial, since he is a member of the coalition, but not an American. Know what I mean? It will really throw those Seattle wackos for a loop.

1800 hrs

I am exhausted from my travels. I need to shower and shave with a whole lot of hustle, and fall into bed. My cot is nothing compared with the accommodations I had on my trip: a building with real rooms, with locking doors *and* closets. Did I mention the sheets were starched and wrapped up in plastic until ready for use? It was like a fucking hotel! Makes my tent seem like a dump!

21 Sept 2300 hrs

Had another awesome day today, except for the constant attacks from Sergeant First Class Morrison. I had a radio interview scheduled, and she did everything she could to see that it didn't happen; however, I pulled it off without a hitch. I was on for forty-five minutes in the Seattle market, which, during morning drive time, is quite a coup. First Lieutenant Furlani also was on for a little bit. Having been an exchange student in Seattle, he was able to speak eloquently on both America and Italy's role in the war on terror. After the interview, we went over to his building (35) and had pasta with fresh clams, prepared by another Italian soldier. Captain Olson, from my office, accompanied me to ensure that I didn't get into any trouble.

22 Sept 2200 hrs

I haven't been to the pool in what seems like forever. Isn't that strange? All the places I've gone and things I've seen here in Iraq, and I still have time to swim once in a while. Today we were hauling our new satellite uplink system up and down from the roof to set it up in different places. It was really good training, but was hot as balls up on the roof all day long. Plus the roof was full of metal bars and things that amounted to anti-personnel emplacements. Staff Sergeant Mann put his hands down to move from one level to another and he ended up with fiberglass slivers in his hands and ass.

23 Sept. 2330 hrs

All day again with the uplink equipment. Finally we got a lock with the satellite up in the sky. That was a great feeling, knowing that we got this quarter of a million dollar piece of gear to work. Now we can beam stories and interviews directly back to the states or around the world.

24 Sept. 1615 hrs

Made it to the pool today. All the other pool rats thought I had been killed on a mission. I did my first broadcast back to Central Texas this morning, which was really exciting. All went well except for all the officers milling about, generally getting in the way. One of them said "fuck" over an open microphone back to the hub in Atlanta. It was so funny. The first thing they teach you in broadcasting school is to always assume the microphone is on. If I had done that, it would have been very, very bad for me.

I killed two beetles in my tent today. The big huge ones like you see in the mummy movies. It took an awful lot of pressure to crack their bodies. I mean I stepped on it with my shoe and I had to press down hard. Amazing how strong they were.

I'm at the Aussie pool again. There is a concert and comedy show here tonight featuring, of course, Australians. Some Aussie girl just came over and asked if I was doing paperwork here at the pool. I said no, I am just writing in my journal. Her name is Wendy and she is an Australian Air Force reservist from Brisbane. She enjoys competing in triathlons back home. Here in Baghdad she swims and runs whenever she can. I had my picture taken with her, since she went out of her way to be friendly with me.

25 Sept 0900 hrs

The concert last night rocked. I really miss my wife, though; this was something she would have enjoyed over here. I spent the night hanging out with Specialist Franks and 1st. Lt. Roberto Furlani, the close talking Italian. He has become my new best buddy. The show featured the Aussie Air Force band, a hilarious comedian, and of course, a slutty MC. Her body was definitely a sight for sore eyes for many a soldier over here. There was also a band called the **"Choir Boys"** (*www.choirboys.net*). The next was a total blast! I had Kiver-Aid to drink all night long. That is what Roberto calls my hydration technique. I called my wife afterward; she started to cry because she missed me so. She also got a little mad because she thought I was having too much fun over here. I did have a blast, and made sure Roberto took lots of photos of everyone involved.

I am out at the rifle range right now. I came out with two other journalists in my office who are having difficulties qualifying with their weapons. Some people don't take this stuff seriously because they think they will never have to use it. I guess there are those who will always remain at the rear with the gear; however, where is the rear in today's war? Regardless, I am here to try to help them. Marksmanship is a combination of many things: if you're off with just one thing, your bullet will always go astray. When you need to kill someone, well, then you need to kill someone.

26 Sept 1700 hrs

I had a huge blowout with my supervisor this afternoon. It left me emotionally exhausted. I have been doing well in my professional development course online though. I am going to watch some episodes of *The Simpsons* on DVD tonight—a great distraction from work.

27 Sept 0700 hrs

I have been up since 0330 hrs. First, I went for a run around the palace lake. Then I went in to the office, talked to the wife, and read the news online. I have some more filming to do this morning for my Italian buddies; they are going to owe me so big! I have been filming this huge documentary for the Italian commander so that he can take it back to their military academy to show the students or whatever.

28 Sept 0900hrs

Last night, Birmingham and I stopped by Building 85 to see my buddy, Major Chisom, of the 420th Engineers. He asked if I would like to play darts with him sometime. I said one doesn't play darts, one throws darts, you bohemian! Today we finished our satellite uplink training. I am the only broadcaster on the team; the other three soldiers are newspaper journalists who are just along for the ride. The system is pretty cool; the dish puts out tons of microwave energy. We were joking that Zarcawi, the terrorist, should get a set for himself, then we would film him. But the best part would be telling him to stand right in front of the dish; then it would cook his brains.

29 Sept 0900 hrs

I just finished a quick shoot with some soldiers from the National Guard in my home state of Washington. One of them I actually knew from years gone by. The story was about convoy safety and reactions to enemy contact. Although just work, it was nice to be with guys who speak and think similar to me because of where we are all from. The story is important though, as I am using it as part of a safety briefing for the soldiers I work with. That way, we can all be safe when we are out on the roads of Iraq.

Right now I am at the alterations shop getting my combat patch sewn on the sleeve of my uniform. In the army, having a combat patch is a big deal; it tells others at a glance that you have been in a war zone and what unit you were with. For those who pay attention to military history or current events, you can quickly determine where that person served. With the up-tempo in deployments, it seems everyone will be earning their patch. Consequently, it wouldn't be cool to be the only soldier without one. So this is a big deal for me right now and a proud day as well, knowing that I have earned the right to wear this for my country.

30 Sept 2200 hrs

Daylight saving time for us here in Iraq. I don't know why we are going on it a month sooner than the rest of the world, but whatever, it is an extra hour of sleep, I suppose. The last two nights, I had dinner with the Italians. Tonight I attended two different parties/social functions here in camp. I am very tired right now, so I will tell you more tomorrow. Oh, one more thing; a soldier was killed today by an incoming rocket. I can't believe I almost forgot to mention that. Sleep…

1 Oct 0900 hrs

As promised, here are the details. A soldier was killed yesterday by a rocket. A singular tragedy in a whole sea of such things. He was retiring after twenty years in the army. He had put in his retirement papers here and was going home within a week. My wife asked me how I felt about it. I said I have no emotional investment in death here. I'm living in one of the most violent places on earth. Every time I hear an explosion or see a black cloud of smoke, I know that someone was killed or injured. Yet I feel so detached from the reality of it all. I think that even if someone I work with were to be killed, it couldn't bother me now. Death is just the cost of doing business. I am not callus, just trying to prevent overdrawing on my emotional savings account as it were.

My wife asked today if I would be home for Christmas. The answer was no. She didn't like hearing that at all. Our anniversary is the first week of November. That is where my emotional energies go, to the pain of separation.

When I get angry, I direct it at know-nothing hippies who write letters to the editor like they know what is really going on here. I try to take the time to write rebuttals when I see these things in the paper. Unfortunately, it is like holding back the tide. I called one man in my hometown about his letter. Don Wall is the man's name. He is an old family friend/acquaintance of my father's. He wouldn't accept my call; his wife was screening for him. A true coward hides behind his poison pen when confronted with the facts. I'm starting to feel like one of those old Vietnam vets who gets angry when people talk about their war. How dare they!

Also in the paper was a column from some punk in my hometown, talking about how he feels threatened by Saudi

Arabia while living in Eastern Washington. I called to talk to his ass, but he wasn't in. He also declined the opportunity to respond to me via email. I just put my head down on the table and felt really discouraged for the first time. The mission and cause is just, yet it will take another 9-11 to remind Americans about what is going on in the world between good and evil. I feel like I am trying to yell over a passing freight train to people on the other side while I can only see them through the spaces between the moving cars. There are so many positive things going on here in Iraq and no one at home knows anything about it. I need to go to the pool. Time to pull myself up by my own bootstraps.

2 Oct 0640 hrs

Back out at the M-16 range. Not because I have to; I want to be here right now, shooting, even if it is just practice. I have a huge ceremony to narrate tomorrow, since I am the only broadcaster around. Apparently, no one else in the army can talk and read at the same time. Unfortunately, I was trying to be sarcastic, but it ended up being true. Regardless, this ceremony tomorrow is very important. It is a naturalization ceremony for soldiers and marines who are not American citizens. The list of names I have to pronounce is brutal. I have never seen a collection of names like this ever before. This event will be broadcast on Fox News, CNN, and the highlights shown on all of the hometown markets as well. I cannot make any mistakes! On top of this pressure, my sleep rhythm is all jacked up right now because of going on daylight saving a whole month before what I am used to. This morning I went swimming in the pool at 0100 hrs. The water was very warm, complemented by the perfect air temperature.

1700 hrs

Still very hot this afternoon. I am sitting in my lawn chair on my front porch outside my tent, as opposed to the front porch that I have inside my tent. Insert laugh here. The ceremony is tomorrow at 1300 hrs, no mistakes!

Tuesday I will be flying to Karbala with the Italians to visit their soldiers based in that area of the country. I have been here at Camp Victory too long. Time to hit the road again.

3 Oct 2200 hrs

Where do the days go? The ceremony went very well. We made thirty-four soldiers and marines into U.S. citizens. After that, we interviewed several of them on the satellite uplink back to their hometowns. Earlier in the day I met Oliver North and was able to speak with him for about ten minutes, which was a real privilege.

4 Oct 0715 hrs

Just another manic Monday. Went swimming at 0200 hrs while my laundry was washing in the machine. Then I went for a run around the lake. It is so hard to try to get into any routine when your schedule and location can change all the time. Heard last night that I may be heading to Fallujah in a couple of weeks for the big expected offensive.

1600 hrs

Well, I'm officially having my worst day ever. My immediate supervisor, whom I thought was my friend, is not recommending me to the promotion board for sergeant. Not completely unexpected though. I don't fit nicely into the military box like some people would like. For me, the mission has always come first. Screw protocol and tradition. I want to get things done. I am always getting yelled at for talking to generals. It is really funny, 'cause you know what? They are people too. They always enjoy talking to soldiers. It is their staff that gets upset, because if you talk directly to the general, then the colonel has nothing to do; however, I have two things going for me: I am still alive, and still getting paid.

5 Oct 0815 hrs

Back at the LZ, waiting for a helicopter. How many hours of my youth have I wasted waiting at these places? But this is what I'm comfortable with, doing missions. I'm headed to Karbala for the day, as I mentioned before. It is just for the day; I wish it was for a month—anything to get the hell away from my chain of command. I spoke to that asshole, Staff Sergeant M— this morning. I swallowed my pride, which wasn't easy, and apologized for whatever I did to make him so mad. That diffused the situation a lot. He was very angry when he came into the office, but after half an hour of sporadic conversation, I learned why he was really angry: his tour had been extended by thirty days, and that pissed him off. He hates everyone from III Corps, which is all of us. He calls them III Corps douche bags! He is a reservist from 3rd Army, so he is anxious to get home. He may be coming back again, as soon as April.

I have a pocketful of U.S. flags, which I am going to trade with the Italian and Bulgarian soldiers I meet today.

The flies are really bothering me this morning. It seems as the weather turns cooler, there are more of these annoying little bastards.

1600 hrs

What a fun trip I had. We visited two different Bulgarian camps today. I must have been the first American soldier they had ever seen; everyone wanted to have their photo taken with me, which made me feel really special. They were also most interested in my M-16. All of them carry the old Soviet style AK-47, which I was interested in holding as well. It was a great afternoon of cultural exchange. I was able to get lots of Bulgarian uniform patches for my flags too. We took a convoy through the city in order to visit the mayor and city council. The convoy was a cross between Indy car racing and a demolition derby. We made it safely to the city hall; I guess that's what it is called. They had prepared a large spread for us to eat. The very first thing that happened was that some men brought a live sheep in the yard for us to pet and look at. Then they killed it right there in front of us. Apparently, this lamb was to be the main course, to go with all the other food that was prepared. Well, at least we knew the meat was fresh. Over lunch I struck up a conversation with a Shia man who spoke very good English. I asked him what he thought about our presidential election. He asked his friends in Arabic and then replied to me saying that all five of them would vote for Bush because he does what he says and says what he does. He also added that five members of his family had been sent to prison during Saddam's rule. None of them were ever heard from again, and he presumes that they are dead in a mass grave somewhere. Further, they want the American soldiers to stay here for a while. "We are thirsty for democracy after thirty-five years of murder and torture." Hearing this, I asked what he thought about Saddam as a man. "Goddamn him; I spit upon the graves of Uday and Quasi. Killing Saddam would only bring him rest. Send him to Abu Ghraib to be tortured for the rest of his life, until he dies of old age." Why can't we hear from guys like this on the nightly news back home? Talk about a public relations coup! From one Arab to another, it doesn't get any stronger than what this man said about Saddam.

6 Oct 1700 hrs

I took care of tons of administrative details and busy work today, pushing missions through the request pipeline, catching up on emails and personal correspondence. Trying to use the chain of command is not as easy as you would think. Now you can't talk face to face. Everyone wants emails, and to be CC'd, and stupid shit like that. For someone as creative as me, it presents a huge roadblock. I am the two-phone-call, one-handshake type of businessman. Look me in the eye, and we have an agreement.

I just tried to extend and stay longer here in Iraq. I wouldn't mind staying another two, three months or so. I really want to see the aftermath of the elections. I asked Sergeant Major Parris, from my office, if I could extend; he said no. Lieutenant General Metz wants everyone who came over with III Corps to go home at about the same time. Some "no man left behind" thing. I'm not the only soldier who wants to extend. It makes sense to keep us here. We already know our jobs and the lay of the land here. We would be very valuable to the gaining unit, since we have been here for months already. It would spare some other soldier and their loved ones the pain of separation, at least for a while. It would also save the Department of Defense money. Same soldier stays; no need to send a new one over or bring an old one home. Of course, there are other considerations, like my wife filing for divorce were I to volunteer to stay here longer. No, I'm not kidding—I'm sure she would—nor would I blame her. Also, do I want to tempt fate and dare the terrorists to try to kill me a second time around? My friend, who is a major general in the reserves, advised me not to extend. A friend of his did and was killed shortly after his extension began. Alas, like Patrick Henry said, "I regret that I have but one life to give for my country."

7 Oct 1500 hrs

Well, I have several trips in the planning stages right now. The first is to Fallujah for the big offensive. This depends upon the green light from the Iraqi president. He says go or no at this point for taking the city by force. Also, I am trying to fly up to Germany to follow wounded soldiers from Iraq to the hospital at Lanstuhl Regional Medical Center. All of the appropriate medical folks have given tacit approval, yet the remaining hurdle is—you guessed it—Sergeant First Class Morrison. I swear, if they put half as much effort into winning the war as they do restricting my journalistic desires, we would all be home by know. Fuck me running! The last trip would be to Rome. The Italians would like me to come and produce the video that I have been collecting footage of here in Iraq. I'm sure it won't happen, but it never hurts to try, and try again.

1800 hrs

Spent the afternoon filming soldiers giving shout outs for specific NFL games coming to a Jumbotron near you. It was really funny watching people clown in front of the camera. Many people really freak out. I coach them, but when the red light goes on and you say "action," they go wild!

8 Oct 2000 hrs

I had a big fight with one of my only good friends here today. First Lieutenant Furlani, the close talking Italian, gave me some blank DVDs. Well, I used them, but he then decided he wanted them back. Well, I couldn't give them back, because they were used. I told him he would have to wait until I could get to the store. He got all mad and tried to pull rank on me. It is hard to be buddies with someone who is in charge. I got all mad as well. I went over to his building to give back what I could. He tried to apologize, but I stuck to my guns, and stormed out. If there is one thing I can do well, it is throw a tantrum.

9 Oct 1200 hrs

High noon. It is so cloudy here today that I could classify it as cool outside. Astounding, to see real clouds in the sky. It looks just like Seattle.

2030 hrs

It has been raining since we last spoke. Real rain, with lots of huge lightening bolts in the sky. I have never seen such huge collections of electricity flashing through the night sky, illuminating the landscape. I grabbed a cigar, went outside to the porch, and smoked while consuming the beverage of my choice. Sometimes I still can't believe where I am in the world. With the clouds and rain today, it didn't even break a hundred degrees. I was freezing! It is amazing how the human body can adjust to different climates, as I have been forced to do here in Iraq.

10 Oct 0930 hrs

Last night I called my hometown FM station to request a song. I spoke with the "Breakfast Boys," Dave and Ken. They asked me if I knew who won the Red Sox game, since I was eleven hours ahead of them. Already ninety-five degrees, no clouds, no rain; all has been dried up from last night already. Looks like another hot one today. I wonder what the *Farmers' Almanac* would have to say about the weather here today. I have to prepare the Italian documentary for export to Rome. I had a great run around the lake last night and then a refreshing swim after that. Back home in Washington, it's getting to be pumpkin picking season. Although I prefer the heat, the rain was a welcome relief, and almost exquisite in nature. The Italians are insisting that I put the footage on tapes as well as on DVDs. Sometimes these Europeans... I tell you, they forget all about the two world wars.

1500 hrs

I just awoke from my afternoon siesta. I was dreaming of winter fun on the streets of my hometown, sledding down a specific hill, in fact. All of the people in the dream were friends from my elementary and high school days—one girl from high school, in particular. I really love my subconscious sometimes, helping me relax by escaping for a few minutes now and then. Unfortunately, I was awakened by a large explosion. Reality!

What a fucking drag. I was all wrapped up in that great dream about home and then the terrorists went and ruined it with their car bomb. I can see these sorts of events affecting my sleep upon my return to America.

11 Oct 2000 hrs

Had some very heavy discussion with my wife today. She took the time and great pains to point out all of my faults. Needless to say, it crowded out all other things I did today. Actually, I am very depressed about it right now. Sometimes it seems the easy thing to do would be running right out in the middle of the road to commit suicide by terrorist. I must admit, there have been times when depression has hit me really hard; nothing that has lasted very long, but when it hits, it hits hard, and puts me down for a few hours at a time. No one would ever suspect it of me either. I am always joking around and am never one to take things seriously. I think if I told someone I was depressed, they would look at me, waiting for the punch line to double them over in laughter. At times it is very hard to remain stoic.

12 Oct 1000 hrs

The Italian Lieutenant Colonel Pannitzi told me something new today. He said, "You have a face of bronze." He continued by explaining that in the course of filming for them, they have watched me interact with and film many dignitaries without fear or confusion. Thus, the bronze face, adding, "You are very brave to do such a thing." Both wonderful comments. Now, if I could only get some support like this from my fellow Americans, instead of having to rely upon the kindness of coalition soldiers.

13 Oct 1900 hrs

I filmed lots of holiday greetings today. To explain how this works, here is how its goes. The soldier comes up, gets in front of the camera and is supposed to give a formal introduction, including name, rank, unit of assignment, and hometown media market. Then they pause three seconds, then start talking, as if their wife or mother is now watching. Many soldiers just don't understand at all, even after getting the briefing about what we want them to do. I will say, "Cut, stop the camera," and ask them, "Do you like your family?" Usually they say yes. Well, why don't you sound like you care about them? It is so funny, but sad at the same time. Some people just don't ever get it right. This leaves me no choice but to put their footage on the cutting room floor. Their families never get to hear from them because they were such poor camera subjects.

14 Oct 2345 hrs

I had three different stories to edit today. As luck would have it, they all had the same deadline, so I am in the midst of a college all-nighter. To make matters worse, we had to be linked with the satellite at 0400 hrs this morning. After we were done, I was on the computer up in the palace. Major Kerrigan was on the phone complaining about others, expecting him to jump through hoops for media relations. Here is the really funny part; he said to the other person on the phone, "I once had to get up at 8:00 A.M. to go pick up someone at the landing zone." Specialist Joyce and I could barely contain our laughter and rage upon hearing this comment. Imagine what a comment like that could do the morale of the enlisted soldiers if they heard officers complaining about having to get up at the God awful 0800 hrs. Well, I better get back to my work and then try to sleep a couple of hours right here at my desk.

15 Oct 2100 hrs

Had another 0400 hrs shoot back to Texas this morning. The majority of the troops in this part of Iraq are from Fort Hood, including the overall command and control element. Consequently, the local stations there always want to interview people and air the stories that I produce over here. I suffered some acid burns on my hands this morning. I opened a new box of AA batteries for my wireless microphones. It was dark, so I didn't notice the corrosion in time. The acid from the batteries leaked all over my hands. The burn was very deep, since the skin absorbs the acid before it comes back up to the surface. Once I realized what was happening, I threw the batteries into the palace moat from the third floor balcony where I was; let the fish deal with them. It turns out the batteries were cheap knock-offs made in China. Apparently, our office couldn't find any Duracells. Who do you suppose was responsible for this? Sergeant First Class Morrison. When I told her what happened to my hands, she appeared to be completely disinterested. Big surprise there, right? By the time the shoot was done, it was 0900 hrs, meaning I had been awake for thirty-one hours. I was only able to sleep four hours, as I had work to do in the afternoon.

My favorite shopping and dining areas in the Green Zone were blown up by suicide bombers this week. In fact, I was planning on going down there to pick up a painting of my wife the day after the bombing. But as of now, the areas are closed. It makes me so angry, because I know it is not the poor Iraqis trying to make a living who are responsible; it is the fucking pagans who want everyone in the country to ride a donkey while wearing a burqa. I do know the salesman's name and where his house is in the zone, so I will try to track him down to see if my painting survived. Hopefully, he did as well.

16 Oct 0700 hrs

I'm out at the range again. I love coming out here to shoot my rifle. There is a soldier sitting across from me whose name is McKeever. He is loud, obnoxious, and funny. It must all be in the name. I'm sitting here, and it is like listening to me talking. It is silly how similar this guy is to me.

17 Oct 1338 hrs

I just won an office pool. Our wayward journalist, Specialist Birmingham, went on a mission with Captain Olson and somehow ended up in the Green Zone for a couple of days. She had until 1200 hrs to make it home today, or face unspecified action. Last night we formed a pool with everyone, putting in a dollar and picking what time they thought she would return. I picked the closest time without going over; in fact, I was off by only fourteen minutes. I won five dollars and some pogs, which is cardboard change that Staff Sergeant Mattox put in the pot. He said he didn't have any other money. I spent my winnings on chips and dip for the office, because the army frowns upon personal winnings from gambling.

18 Oct 0800 hrs

I had a mission to Al-Ramadi this morning, but it was canceled because of conditions in the city. Apparently, the powers that be deemed it was too dangerous to travel there today. Really... danger in a war zone? For once it was not my bosses, but First Lieutenant Furlani's. I never would have guessed. The fact that the mission was canceled pissed me off! Not only do I prefer danger and adventure, I doubt anyone will be interested in pictures of my bunk, which is what I will be taking, since I didn't make the trip.

I went to the Iraqi market here on post today and picked up two paintings I had done. The first was of me standing in front of a helicopter with my camera and weapon. A very cool picture. The second one was a gag gift for Private First Class Dubee. He had this man crush on a male professional wrestler. We managed to get a digital shot of Dubee standing next to a poster of his man crush. So we printed it off and took it to the painter to have it done. This picture is fucking hilarious. We will give it to him at his going away party.

2000 hrs

I encountered a special kind of aggravation at dinner tonight. Major Duck, who I know from Fort Hood, asked me why I hadn't been attending some sensitive briefings about civilians who had escaped from their Iraqi captors. I said I hadn't heard about them. "Bullshit," he replied. "I always tell Lieutenant Colonel Baggio about these things." The issue, as it turns out, was about one prisoner specifically. It seems a Canadian citizen of Kurdish origin was kidnapped here in Iraq. She had been working as a translator. The kidnappers had been in direct contact with her father in Canada to arrange for a ransom. When negotiations broke down, she took it upon herself to escape. After doing this, she ended up at one of our gates, and was taken into custody. After that she was flown north to Balad and then to Germany and points beyond. When she left, so did my chance for a photo on the cover of *TIME* with the soldiers who found her, or any other possibilities. Once again, the journalists were screwed by those above them. What an opportunity. To top it off, there was a Canadian journalist with her on the helicopter, so he got the whole scoop and posted it in the *National Post*. I am so angry I could eat glass! When I related the details to the other journalists I work with, they were equally irate.

19 Oct 1700 hrs

The rest of this week I will be caught up with a prison abuse trial that is taking place here at Camp Victory. One of the infamous Abu Ghraib suspects is going to bat. This evening I will watch *Beavis and Butthead* to help get me into the proper mindset for the trial and what these soldiers are accused of.

20 Oct 0600 hrs

I have to go outside the wire to pick up some journalists who want to cover the court proceedings. This is a fairly simple yet dangerous process. You drive out onto the highway and meet your reporter, who has been dropped off by someone else; however, the area is prime car bomber territory. Soldiers have been killed out here before, so it is best to keep your eyes peeled and act before you have to react to an explosion.

0700 hrs

Waiting outside the courthouse with my coworkers and the reporter I picked up. Here is what happened when we were outside the fence. I drove out there in a regular Ford Explorer with Specialist Birmingham. She, as usual, did nothing to provide security, just wandered around aimlessly. I, however, had my rifle lying across the hood of the vehicle, scanning the highway for any sign of trouble from the passing motorists. A Muslim women dressed in black from head to toe began approaching the car. I leveled my rifle at her and commanded her to stop. She did this while removing her head scarf. Underneath she was no Arab women at all, but actually a very cute blond, who identified herself as a reporter for the BBC from the Vienna office. Well, raise my rent, what a great disguise. We all hopped in the car and hauled ass back to the base. During the drive she explained that she dressed like that in Baghdad so no one would realize she was a westerner. It really fooled me to the point where, if she had kept coming without removing her disguise, I would have shot her. She believed me, as well she should. When we arrived at the courthouse, she took off the rest of her robe. Several of the soldiers really liked her physical appearance as a whole. It didn't really appeal to me; she was way too thin. We did engage in a lively debate about the war as a whole. She refused to acknowledge that there are any positive stories taking place here, even though I have personally seen schools, electric grids, and water purification plants being built by Iraqi labor and contractors. She feels it is all Halliburton and company doing everything here in Iraq. Lucky for her she had a cute face and a lovely British accent, or things could have gotten ugly. I simply can't believe some people's total lack of respect for reality.

Things happen right in front of them, yet they explain them away to suit their own agendas.

0833 hrs

I'm sitting in the courtroom awaiting the court martial to begin. I don't know what the charges are at this point that the defendant, Staff Sergeant Frederick, will be facing. I do feel sorry for the soldiers who get into trouble over these sorts of accusations here in Iraq. There are very bad people in Iraq who want to hurt us. I feel these people deserve whatever happens to them; however, on the other hand, it is law and order that separates us from the animals that behead other human beings and videotape it for the world to see. I guess what I mean is, I sympathize with the situations that any American soldier is placed in that allows for the opportunity for a war crime to occur. I mean, God only knows what I would do if faced with similar circumstances. I hope I would do the hard thing; that is, make the right decision, instead of talking the easy road out. Regardless, America has a system of laws and we must follow them or end up like the animals we must defeat.

By the way, the courtroom where I am right now is the same one in which Saddam made his initial appearance. Court has not started on time. The judge isn't ready yet. In other news, my wife said she mailed my anniversary present. I don't have any idea what it could be; she did say she spent all day working on it. Who knows what it is?

0914 hrs

The judge is here and we are ready to begin. The accused Staff Sergeant Frederick has entered a guilty plea to several charges. He is one of the soldiers allegedly responsible for creating the naked human pyramid at the prison. The blame game is beginning. The prosecution, in their opening statement, is laying all of the blame on Staff Sergeant Frederick. He was the NCOIC on the nightshift in the prison. The defense is spreading the blame around, basically saying the climate created in the prison was not conducive to good order and discipline. Many different kinds of people came in out of the prison: CIA, FBI, DOD, Special Forces. Staff Sergeant Frederick had to deal with all of these folks. If I were on the jury for this trial, it seems to be a very convincing argument. There is no jury by the way; it is only the military judge who will decide and impose sentence.

Staff Sergeant Frederick is entering a guilty plea to several charges. This process involves him stipulating to the facts and explaining what he did and how that was wrong. Many of his statements sounded like defense arguments. In fact, the judge kept stopping him and asking for more clarification and explanation. He was still assigning blame to others, as well as himself, in several instances. In fact, the judge told him several times, "You can only plead guilty to a crime if you think you are guilty. I cannot, in good faith, let you plead guilty if you feel you are not guilty of these crimes." Everyone seemed to pay strict attention to these particular statements by the judge. Over and over he stressed that he did not know who was in charge above him in the prison. "Ghosts" would bring prisoners in and say, "Work them over or soften them up." Staff Sergeant Frederick heard these statements and acted as he though he should. Specialist Joshua Joyce, another journalist from my office, wrote down the same quotes from the judge that I did regarding the guilt of Staff Sergeant Frederick, even though he was watching from another room. During the next recess, I spoke to Sergeant First Class Morrison about what the judge said. She replied, "You got the quotes wrong, the judge never said that." I told her I wrote it down, I was right there, but she insisted I was wrong. I was in the courtroom and she was watching on closed circuit; how could she have missed it? Or how could two other journalists make the same mistake word for word? I am starting to feel that the quick fix is to assign blame for this and be done with it, regardless if justice is served. How far up and down the chain does this go, if at all? Perhaps these defendants should be allowed to call high ranking officials as witnesses. Several times the defense has tried to call senior members of the military to testify, and the requests have been denied by the sitting judge.

21 Oct 0700 hrs

The Red Sox won! As a journalist, I am very upset right now, because the World Series was only four games. I easily could have attended every one. When they go seven games, it gets expensive. I had been to the American League championship series when the Mariners played the Yankees.

0924 hrs

The court accepted Staff Sergeant Frederick's guilty plea yesterday. Today is the sentencing phase. Both sides will call witnesses to bolster their particular claims. The defense has presented testimony from several medical experts. I am not sure what they were trying to prove. It seemed that the defendant came out looking like an average guy, who could be any one of us. Not really very compelling at all. One witness who really helped the defense, in my opinion, was the company commander. He testified via teleconference from the U.S. He talked about the horrible conditions for those working at the prison and also the presence of "ghosts," which confused the soldiers he was responsible for. The defense attorney asked him what he would do if presented with this mission again, given the benefit of hindsight. "I would refuse the mission based on what I know now." Silence in the courtroom. I don't see how these soldiers can be sent to jail when their own commander openly acknowledges the problems the prison environment presented.

1100 hrs

The prosecution called an Iraqi whom the prosecution alleges was one of those abused under Staff Sergeant Frederick's watch. They also said this was the man who was physically assaulted by Staff Sergeant Frederick. His testimony did not seem genuine to me. It was coached and very leading; the translator did not help much either. Plus, anyone in this prison during the war is a bad guy who I would not trust in the least bit.

1300 hrs

During the recess, I met a journalist who works for Reuters in New Delhi, India. It will give me a very interesting perspective being here at the trial and then reading the tripe put out over the Internet. We shall see.

1445 hrs

The prosecution's closing argument was cold and brutally honest. They presented many of the photographic images we are used to seeing, plus many I had not seen before, because of their sensitive nature. The defense objected many times to remarks and theories put forth by the prosecution during their closing arguments.

The defense attorney, Mr. Meyers, spoke eloquently and extemporaneously, with no notes or Power Point slides. He was convincing, and very certain of a wider conspiracy than just his client. He demanded accountability from the officers at the prison and those higher up, insisting that although his client had confessed, he was not alone in the blame for the problems.

1530 hrs

I just scored an awesome interview with Staff Sergeant Frederick himself. He came over to the box where I was. I identified myself as an army journalist, but assured him I was speaking as a soldier and an American only. I asked him why he did these things in the first place.

"I was so alone, we were alone, and no one cared what we did to the prisoners. We were doing what the CIA and others asked us to do."

Did you strike that man who testified against you?

"I punched a man who was in the prison, but it was not the one who testified today in court. I didn't speak up and say anything because I want this to be over as quick as possible so I can return to my wife and children."

What do you think about your chain of command?

"I thought someone would speak up and say they knew what was going on. Unfortunately, everyone invoked their right to remain silent. Everyone knew what was going on. The things that occurred before I got there were no different than what I was involved in. As long as no one died, I thought it would be all right."

Staff Sergeant Frederick did have it tough working at the prison: long workdays, no rest, getting shot at by a prisoner with a smuggled weapon. Surely, any one of us might have reacted in the same way; however, he knew what he did was wrong, regardless of who else knew about it. He had a responsibility for his own actions, and he was also in charge of the actions of others. I wonder how far up the chain of command this goes. Staff Sergeant Frederick was sentenced to ten years in prison in court today. Because of a pretrial agreement, it will be reduced to eight years with time served already.

My overall conclusions about the case of Staff Sergeant Frederick are that in my conversation with him, he came across as very likable, but not too bright. In fact, what I told people around me was this, "I like him, but I wouldn't let him mow my lawn, because I am afraid he might hurt himself." I think he was the victim of horrible legal advice. I didn't believe he was guilty of all the charges he pled to. By going through a trial, I believe things would have gone much better for him in the long run. As for the government's position, I feel that he and the other enlisted soldiers currently charged are being used by the government to assign blame and be done with it. As I said earlier, justice is not being done here. It is just the quickest way to wash our hands of the situation. It is horrific that an American soldier has to pay with eight years of his life. For what? Because he made prisoners get naked and put underwear on their heads? These are the same people who killed a U.S. prisoner (Matthew Maupin). These are also the people attacking U.S. soldiers and beheading civilians. Where is the common sense in this whole issue? I can't believe the liberals within our government were able to get these kids sent away to prison for what seemed to be less than serious actions.

22 Oct 2000 hrs

Went for a run this morning on my usual route, complete with swim at the pool. While out running, it seemed that there was a dense fog in the air. It turned out to be a dust storm. The particles were so fine that they simply remained suspended in the air, just like volcanic ash. I don't really know where the dust came from.

We didn't have any severe winds in this area; it just rolled in from somewhere else. The pool water had a layer of topsoil floating on top as well. That didn't stop me from taking a refreshing dip at all.

23 Oct 2300 hrs

Attended a conference in the palace today. It was a meeting for all of the foreign leaders who have soldiers here in Iraq. The meeting was pretty boring, from a news angle, just talking about how to work together and help one another. One fact that I can't share with you, but I can allude to, is there are countries with personnel who are not officially part of the coalition. They are providing great services, but because of the delicate political situations in their home countries, it is not seen as an official contribution; however, if I could tell you, it would be very surprising. Buy me a beer! In the evening there was a social event. I did short interviews with several military leaders, getting them to say in English and their own language how they feel about the war on terror and such. One interview was with Major General Weber, USMC chief of staff for all of Iraq. I had to put the microphone up his uniform; much to my surprise, he was not wearing a brown t-shirt underneath. Very hairy and sweaty, and totally awkward for me. I said quickly, "Laundry day, General?" "I don't wear t-shirts," was his reply. While I was setting up the interview with the Korean general, I noticed he had a beer in his hand. I took the can from him so it wouldn't be seen on TV. Looking for a garbage can and seeing none, I turned to my boss, Lieutenant Colonel Baggio, and said, "Please throw this away for me, sir." He scampered off to do it. It was priceless. Lieutenant O'Neil witnessed the whole exchange.

24 Oct 1700 hrs

I went to play flag football today; we have an organized league here, but unfortunately, I had to leave for a story before we got to play our first game. I had to go film the EOD robots in action. These videos were so the manufacturers could show the purse holders at the Pentagon what their robots were doing in Iraq. Translation: buy more of my robots, because they are being used in this video. There were several different kinds that were being considered for future buys.

25 Oct 0800 hrs—birds

I am waiting on the flight line for the helicopter to take me to Al Kut for Kazakhstan's Independence Day. Many from Building 35 are going on this trip with me today as well. The helicopter is approaching from the distance. Time to jam.

2100 hrs

Crazy times today. While we were flying away from Baghdad, our helicopter was attacked by a flock of birds. It all happened so quickly, my glasses were covered with bird guts and pieces of bone. The helicopter lost power in the left engine. We lurched dangerously over and to the right; I was sure we were going to crash, and I was quickly seeing the news article in my mind as we were plummeting down to earth. In a split second, the pilot recovered just in time. We turned around and headed to the Green Zone to make an emergency landing. When we landed and powered down, I was able to talk to the crew and figure out exactly what had happened. Three birds struck the aircraft. The first hit the copilot through the left side; the second hit the left side gunner's weapon, splattering all over me and the inside of the aircraft; and the third was sucked into the air intake of the engine, which was the cause of our descent and loss of power. In fact, pieces of bird bone were imbedded in my safety goggles. Imagine losing your sight because of a bird. The bird responsible for the power loss was still intact. I put it in my carry-on bag to show people back at camp. As a result, my helicopter was officially grounded until the maintenance crews could come and look at it. While waiting for them, several of us walked over to the Pizza Hut and grabbed some food. It was quite a sight, soldiers wearing all their battle rattle with weapons loaded, eating pizza in a parking lot in downtown Baghdad. Amazing, when I think about it. We returned to the flight line about the same time that our replacement helicopter arrived. Our original crew boarded this bird with us, and we were off.

Since we were late for the scheduled events in Al Kut, everything was rushed—the briefings and the lunch. Lunch was a large spread of food, with no seasonings on the lamb or rice. Plain food—didn't these people ever meet Marco Polo? The soldiers from Kazakhstan are a very homogenous bunch from the Central Asian Highlands. I enjoyed the time with them, especially the conversation through the interpreters. Some of them spoke Russian, so I could talk directly to them a little bit.

When all was finished, we went back out to the helicopters, which had been waiting for us all afternoon. What do you suppose happened? One of them was broken right there. Some oil pump in the rear compartment kept blowing when they did the pre-flight maintenance checks. This was the new helicopter we had traded for. Luckily, we always travel with two helicopters. The bad news was we would have to leave half of our party behind. The broken helicopter could make a one-time flight with crew only—no passengers. That way it is only the crews' lives in jeopardy should they go down. Colonel Harrington made the cuts, and I was awarded a seat going home that day. This day has been crazy; all of these events happening around me, yet I keep on trucking. Knock on wood, and I shall go to bed. I need sleep.

26 Oct 2000 hrs

Was told today my jump-off date for Fallujah will be Friday morning after the weekly satellite shoot. My officer in-charge (OIC), Captain Dunkelberger, USMC, tried to get me off the dozer story. I spoke with Colonel Howard, USMC, about that. He called Dunkelberger on the phone and got tacit approval for it. Why? Because Kiver always wins. All joking aside, this will be one of my more dangerous missions to date. I will be on the road for the next two to three weeks, out of touch with the world. I am very excited about getting geared up to go where the actual fighting is taking place. As I am writing, I'm listening to my favorite eighties' songs on the headphones. I took a great long nap this afternoon; that way I can get up early, do laundry, and go for a run. I also need to get my head shaved as well. Hair will be one less thing I have to worry about on my trip. Love you, honey, good night!

27 Oct 1200 hrs

Just chilling in the sun. I'm pretty much off until I leave for my trip on Friday. I have been taking time to write lots of letters to folks back home, should anything happen while I am gone. I have to begin packing in earnest, as well. But right now, right here, I am content to soak up the rays.

28 Oct 1200 hrs

My eye twitch has returned. I leave in the morning, and am all a tingle. I'm sitting in the sun again; gotta keep a nice tan going. There were lots of attacks on our base perimeter last night. A car bomb killed one soldier and injured three. They were National Guardsmen from my home state. I haven't checked to see if I knew them yet. I'm just trying to put away the hurt until sometime in the future, when I can deal with it.

Today I purchased a Seattle Mariners jersey online. The name I had put on the back was "Iraq Veteran." For a small initial investment, I hope people around the league buy me beers next season.

29 Oct 0800 hrs

I have somewhere around two months left on my tour. I learned that my replacement has a name and is a real soldier. I haven't met Sergeant Nelson, but I did meet his colonel from Fort Bragg, who was here this morning on an advance visit. It was very reassuring to know that he is coming. Right now I think I should be leaving sometime between January 10 and 30.

I leave on my extended trip today. I spoke with my wife several times on the phone. She went out drinking last night, hopefully not to forget me. Well, I should think about getting my gear on and leaving my tent for the next month.

2100 hrs

Fallujah, day one. It was a short flight from Baghdad to Fallujah. It is only thirty miles to the west. Our helicopters flew right over Abu Ghraib prison. While waiting on the flight line for our ride, we saw outgoing artillery firing. While we could not see our guns, we heard the round and then saw the smoke plumes rise from the city. I'm sure Al-Jazeera will say that we are killing women and children by the hundreds. Well, I'm real close to it now. In fact, we drove by the dozers I will be filming on our way to our quarters. They are huge steel beasts.

30 Oct 0920 hrs

I slept very well on a bunk bed with a real mattress. Although we are on the front line right now, it is not nearly as rustic as I though it would be. There are phones and Internet just like at any other office I have been in. Right now I am waiting on a marine engineer.

1208 hrs

I just finished eating my lunch on top of a D9 dozer. I am out here with the crews as they perform maintenance on these machines before heading into Fallujah. This afternoon they will be practicing pushing dirt around. My lunch was a ready to eat meal (MRE), with two of the dozer operators eating with me. We were just shooting the shit, so I could get a feel for what sort of an interview to do with them individually. One of these marines is from Cleveland, Ohio. He said he hadn't spoken to his mother in a while, so I handed him my cell phone. He said, "Really?" It was quite a sight to see this young marine talking on a cell phone atop a dozer with the city of Fallujah in the background. Personally, I have never really liked marines, but I may be heading into battle with them, so I better get used to the idea.

A mortar round just landed inside the base, courtesy of the savages in Fallujah. As I am writing this, I'm sitting in the dirt with my back up against the blade of the dozer. To see just how big these things are, go to Caterpillar's homepage and check them out. Don't forget to add on all the armor these have, courtesy of Israel.

2015 hrs

Called home today. As I said, the cell phone works, depending on where you stand. One phrase that I have repeated to my friends and family on the phone is that being here is like starring in your own war movie. Jets are making bombing runs across the sky, artillery is being fired, incoming, outgoing—it is all very surreal. You just get used to it, though, if that is possible. I walk around with confidence that nothing is going to hit me, so therefore it doesn't.

31 Oct 1346 hrs

Happy Halloween! Today I was able to kill lots of time. I walked out to the gun line, where the artillery pieces are set up. The position is about one and a half miles from the camp itself. They have their own secured perimeter to keep the bad guys from crawling in. I came out to do some interviews with the crew members who work here. Their lives seem pretty boring. Live out next to your gun for forty-eight hours, then get one day off. They have to be ready to receive a fire mission at any time. While hanging out, I asked them if I could fire the guns when the opportunity arose. They said that would be fine. Sure as shit, fire missions started coming in. The radio operator screams to the other crew members things like direction, distance, what kind of round to fire, etc. Everyone is running around screaming; it looks like mayhem, but is really very organized. I calmly walked up to the side of the weapon and took the lanyard from a marine. When the non-commissioned officer in charge (NCOIC) yelled fire, I pulled the rope. The 155-MM Howitzer barked with a fury like I had never experienced before. Even with my earplugs in, I felt like I had lost some hearing for sure. After firing, I watched for impact downrange. A few seconds and eight thousand meters later, impact! Some terrorists and their hideout blown away. This happened over and over while I was out there with the marines. These guys are in a reserve unit based in Tennessee. Most of them are from that state, while a few are from Northern Georgia. The downtime may be dull for these warriors, but when the mission comes down, they are all business.

Right now I am sitting on a bench in the camp waiting for a meeting to begin about the voting process in the city of Najaf. A female officer came up to me and asked if Lieutenant Colonel Baggio was my boss. I told her he was, and she beamed and said, "He is so cool." You'll remember, this is the same guy who asked if I was a retard. The nickname we have for him is "Ace." Another of my officers has a nickname; we call him "Sierra Echo." This is from the military phonetic alphabet letters S and E. They stand for the product called "Summer's Eve." This one is my favorite. At this very moment I am in the middle of a meeting, explaining our mission to Najaf, to cover the voter registration process and how it is progressing since the city is relatively calm right now. I am always wary of the stray suicide bomber driving up to places like this whenever I am around. Will have to be extra cautious.

1948 hrs

Just started another meeting, which is a continuation of the first one this afternoon; however, this one features death by Power Point. One interesting fact that I just learned was that the Iraqi election officials were trained in a Latin American country by the United Nations. I can't tell you which country it was.

When I talked to my wife today, she told me that when she was in bed, someone was rubbing her back. She thought it was me, but it turned out to be the cat.

Between these meetings, I had gone back out to the gun line to talk to some more marines and fire a few more rounds, to make sure those left in Fallujah don't get too much sleep. When I walked out there this time, I knew where I was going, because I had been the same way previously. I came into the perimeter at the six o'clock position. I chatted up some more marines, had dinner, and generally just hung out. We had a few more fire missions, much to my enjoyment. The sun had gone down quickly and I had to return for the meeting. I said goodbye and retraced my steps to the perimeter. What I found was the breach in the wire had been closed for the evening, so I was more or less trapped. I returned to the gun and asked the marines how to get out. They didn't know, but told me to go ask the executive officer, or XO. I found him, and he pointed me in the right direction. I walked to the twelve o'clock position and left through the vehicle gate. I asked the guard how to get back to camp. He told me to follow the road, which he said would be two or three miles, and it would get me there. I thanked him and was on my way. I stopped to recon my situation and assess the risks. I was outside the secured area, in the dark, by myself, near Fallujah. Shit! How did this happen? I looked back toward the main camp and determined that if I walked overland, it would be quicker and safer than following the road, which could be populated by all sorts of hobgoblins wearing rags on their heads. I chose to go overland. I stayed close to the gun line perimeter so they would see me. Hello, American soldier; don't shoot, thank you. Once I cleared their position, I walked in a slow, deliberate zigzag pattern, stopping every few meters to listen and watch if I was being followed. It was a painstaking process, and honestly, I was a little scared. Fortunately, I kept my wits about me, and relied on my training and common sense to get me back to civilization. When it was all over, I laughed to myself, realizing I had been alone in the countryside of Iraq.

Photo by Phil Kiver

Dawn Thornton-Kiver, my wife and love.

Photo by Phil Kiver

This was the tent where I slept. These tents were made for ten soldiers of the same sex. Typically, they were never full. There was a tent for females directly behind this one. Bathrooms were just next door.

Photo by Phil Kiver

Crista Birmingham strikes a pose.

Photo by Phil Kiver

From left to right: General DePascale, Lt. Roberto
Furlani. Front to back: Major Periatte, Col.
Harrington, and Col. Amanzhanov.

Photo by Phil Kiver

U.S. Marines preparing for a convoy.

Photo by Phil Kiver

My Black Hawk helicopter that was brought down by the bird strike.

Photo by Phil Kiver

A U.S. soldier was trapped in this rocket attack on Camp Victory. He died in his sleep.

Photo by Phil Kiver

A Shiite father tending his badly burned son who is being transported aboard a U.S. C-130 for medical treatment.

Photo by Phil Kiver

Coalition group in Karbala: SPC Franks is lower right, Col. Harrrington, upper right, General DePascale, center middle. Soldiers not identified are from Kazakhstan.

Photo by Phil Kiver

Three soldiers from my company, HHC III Corp. I rode in that vehicle to Camp Anaconda and back.

Photo by Phil Kiver

Main drag at Camp Victory in Baghdad. Convoy rolling by.

Photo by Phil Kiver

From left: Representatives from Lithuania and Mongolia at a Coalition meeting.

Photo by Phil Kiver

The Iraqi Highway Patrol taking a bandit into custody on Highway One far south of the capitol.

Photo by Phil Kiver

Iraqi Highway Patrolman with a Russian-made heavy machine gun.

Photo by anonymous soldier

I took some time to read my favorite book, ***Les Miserables***, while our luggage was being inspected by customs agents before leaving Iraq.

Photo by anonymous soldier

Lt. Roberto Furlani of the Italian Forces posed with me at a party thrown by the Australians.

Photo by Phil Kiver

Soldiers and locals digging through rubble after suicide bombers blew up an entire city block, killing women and children. This was the event that greatly upset Bigenho.

Photo by anonymous soldier

From left, Senators Nelson of Nebraska, Chambliss of Georgia, me with a weapon, and Kyl of Arizona on Thanksgiving day in Baghdad.

Photo by anonymous soldier

Norm, Major Ali of the Highway Patrol and me with my flight bag, complete with patches from coalition countries.

Photo by Phil Kiver

One of the lions that belonged to Saddam's son, Uday. She was rescued by American troops during the capture of Baghdad.

Photo by Phil Kiver

Looking across the lake to the Joint Visitors Bureau, otherwise known as the hotel where we had parties.

Photo by Phil Kiver

Spc. Joycee, one of my co-workers with the Al-Faw Palace in the background.

Photo by Phil Kiver

Taking orders for pizza in Iraq.

Photo by Phil Kiver

Pizza Hut and the line that follows it at Camp Anaconda. Brand name
fast foods are very popular in a war zone.

Photo by Phil Kiver

Robin Williams signing autographs during photo frenzy on stage.

Photo by Phil Kiver

U.S. bomb-sniffing German shepherd watches Robin Williams
show at Camp Victory.

Photo by Phil Kiver

Sgt. Pippen, one of my co-workers, affectionaely nicknamed, *Hippie*.

Photo by Phil Kiver

First Cavalry Division soldier with *thousand-yard-stare* after loading a wounded child aboard an Australian C-130.

Photo by Phil Kiver

American Black Hawk pilot trying to take a digital photo of his aircraft.

Photo by Phil Kiver

MG Novelli, Italian Forces, in center adjusting his chin strap, is Deputy Commander of the Multi-National Corps in Iraq. He is surrounded by his body guards following a trip I took with them to Karbala.

Photo by Phil Kiver

Norm, a local Iraqi, exchanges greetings with a Utah National Guard Engineer.

Photo by Phil Kiver

Iraqi child posing with shoes I gave him when I covered the completion of the Highway One project. Shoes are in short supply in Iraq and kids are thrilled to receive them.

Photo by Phil Kiver

Christmas tree on the second floor of the Al-Faw Palace where my bosses worked.

Photo by Phil Kiver

A feast of celebration upon completion of the Highway One project. Lamb, vegetables, pita bread, and soda was served on the floor.

Photo by Phil Kiver

Military personell, escort Norm and a group of local Sheiks on an inspection tour upon the completion of Highway One.

Photo by Phil Kiver

Saddam's pool at the palace where I swam until discovering the Aussie pool.

Photo by anonymous soldier

This is the Aussie pool where I spent some pleasant times.

Photo by Phil Kiver

This is the trailer next to the one that took the direct hit. The occupants of this trailer survived.

Photo by anonymous soldier

That's me firing an M4.

Herald/SHAUNA INTELISANO

Kiver reunites with his wife Dawn Kiver
Corps homecoming Friday on Fort Hood.

2315 hrs

I've been on the flight line here in Fallujah for two hours awaiting transportation to Najaf. More time wasted. If this weren't free travel, I might register a complaint.

2 Nov 0305 hrs

Made it to Forward Operating Base (FOB) "Duke." When we were boarding the marine helicopter in Fallujah, I had to back up a Hummer close to the helicopter to unload our gear from the truck to the bird. It was very dark, and the engines were running on the helicopter. We got all the gear in; I took the very last seat, since it is my favorite, and we took off. Captain Dunkelberger didn't think I was on the helicopter. He yelled at Mattox, asking him where I was. Mattox strained his eyes under the green glow of the cabin to see me sitting in the last seat. Apparently, Dunkelberger thought I had driven away in the Hummer instead of getting on the helicopter.

We should be getting transportation on to Najaf later today. Of course, I have another meeting at 1000 hrs to discuss this again! I want to find out if we get four more years of Bush today. I really dislike John Kerry even more so than Clinton. Kerry is a mealy mouthed liberal elitist who thinks he can help the poor. His wife is even worse. Bush, on the other hand, believes in something. Even if others disagree with him, he will not waiver on his beliefs. Plus, I am very supportive of the Bush doctrine of preemptive strikes against those who would attack us. I had a good conversation yesterday with the folks back home at the radio station. Everyone seems to be very supportive of what is going on over here. I hope America does not switch horses in the middle of the race.

1010 hrs

Another fucking meeting and more death by Power Point. To top it off, I am very tired. It is cold and rainy here today. The last thing I want is to get sick on this trip. Although I don't want to be here, this meeting is very interesting. We, the Americans involved in the election process, are actually the founding fathers of a new Iraq. I imagine that Ben Franklin and the rest of those gentlemen encountered the same problems that that we are seeing now. Here are some common examples: illiteracy, mistrust of the process, lack of understanding. What is a political party? What does a vote mean? Who is eligible to vote? The work we will be involved in is very important. The reports of our progress go back to Washington to be read by the president himself.

2126 hrs

Well, I made it to Najaf. They put me and Staff Sergeant Mattox in the back of a seven-ton truck with all our gear and drove us down the highway. It was a little chilly, but being up that high in an open truck provided a great view of the countryside. While driving through town, I was throwing MREs out of the truck to the children on the road. I think a little girl ended up with one; the boy who tried to get to it first fell down in the ditch, which was funny, because females are treated so poorly here. It is nice to see them come out ahead once in a while.

Right now it is raining like you wouldn't believe. I had dinner tonight and it was one of the best ever. The salad bar had all sorts of fresh vegetables and fruits: avocadoes, whole kiwis, and tons of other stuff. I learned that the commanding officer (CO) here is a reservist marine who owns a produce farm in California. He has all the stuff flown in himself for his fellow marines.

After dinner I went and spoke with the marines who are living next to me. They had all been in the battle of the cemetery in Najaf. After talking about that for a little while, they switched topics to abuse of farm animals when they were younger. I guess the marines will talk to just about anyone about anything. I guess when you have seen the kind of action that these young men have, you need to cut loose once in a while.

3 Nov 1919 hrs

Democrats need to shut the fuck up! Republicans have an even larger majority now. Our country has spoken and Bush and his agenda are the choice of the country right now.

This morning we took a trip through Najaf to the local television station to survey their needs and capabilities. It was very interesting for me as a TV journalist to visit an Iraqi station. The employees there really liked my camera, and showed me a catalog that had one they wanted to purchase.

Switching gears a little bit to talk about sex. The phrase to learn today is "six swinging dicks and one monkey pussy." Let me explain. In the mess hall is a marine captain; she is part of the contingent that is working with me. She is cute, I guess, but to these marines she is a goddess. Anyhow, she is surrounded by six male marine officers who are all hanging on her every word. She is obviously enjoying the attention. From far away she looks like a monkey with her eyes set very close together. Oh, most of the officers drooling over her are married, as well.

Here is another bit of camp gossip. It seems one female here was caught *performing* on a fellow marine in a porta-shitter. Now how desperate do you have to be to do that? I asked around and some people wanted to know if it was a clean bathroom? Does it matter? It is a shitter!

4 Nov 1200 hrs

I'm in the waiting room of the governor's complex in the city of Najaf. I'm supposed to get an interview, which will be televised live back to the states. I've been here for over an hour waiting for him. His palace is like Jabba the Hutt's lair: all sorts of nefarious looking characters lurking about; Arab men armed with AK-47s. In the U.S. Army, we don't point guns at people unless we mean to shoot. These pagans do it all the time just walking around. Except for the weapons, it is just like back home waiting on the politicians. I was heavily involved in politics in my previous existence. This guy (the governor) spent the last few years living in Chicago. Apparently, Saddam was not on his Christmas card list. Once we took him down, it was safe for this man to move back. I don't trust the governor, though; his facial hair is thin for an Arab. Look at me, being all ethnocentric. I can't help it; he just looks like a criminal. That's how I avoided jury duty back home. I told the judge I could spot a guilty person just by looking at him.

2200 hrs

Repeat of the monkey show at the chow hall tonight. I spoke with two other female marines who totally knew what was going on and agreed with my assessment.

5 Nov 0930 hrs

I have been on the road for a week now. Times like this make me realize just how much crap I own in the U.S. that I don't need in order to live. I have been living out of a small trunk for a week now. It has everything I need to live and be clothed. When I use something up, I just throw it away, creating space. I tend to be a real pack rat back in the world. This morning I will be going on a convoy to look at voter registration sites throughout Najaf.

1900 hrs

I spent four hours riding in the back of a Humvee through the streets of Najaf and then its twin city, called Kufa. I had my camera on a monopod, which allowed me to have a terrific three hundred sixty-degree view of all the passing action. We stopped a few times to talk to local leaders about what was going on in their neighborhoods. On one stop, we were absolutely mobbed by children, even more so because I had a nice camera. All the children wanted to have their picture taken. The cool thing with digital is that I can take the picture and then immediately show it to them, which causes them to squeal with delight. These types of stops are dangerous as well. It would be a devastating attack if a car bomber were to ram us with all these children around. Every time we stop, we have soldiers who are dedicated to pulling perimeter security and watching out for those of us who have to interact with the public. On one stop, I saw a little girl and really wanted to take her photo. In Arabic I told the boys to get away and pointed my camera at her. One boy came up, threw her down by her hair, and kicked her in the ribs, so I wouldn't be able to photograph her. A marine who saw what happened said all Iraqis down to age ten should be killed if that is how they treat each other. I can't say I don't agree with him. What a bunch of fucking savages. She was thrown to the ground because of ingrained oppression of women, not because of any playground angst.

6 Nov 1000 hrs

I am at the moral welfare and recreation tent right now watching News Night with Aaron Brown. I should be back in Fallujah by Tuesday. Full scale operations have been pushed off until tomorrow. I have taken lots of wonderful photos here. Staff Sergeant Mattox has become obsessed with photographing donkeys on the roadways.

7 Nov 1414 hrs

My mission today was ninety percent planning (ineffective) and ten percent action. We were supposed to go to the governor's mansion again to set up our equipment and test the signal strength and whatnot; however, our command failed us in this endeavor. How? you ask. Oh, it was as simple as not requesting a truck to haul all of our equipment. This really didn't bother me, as it was a pain in the ass to haul all of our gear across town just to set it up and then take it down.

1900 hrs

At the mess hall this evening, it was the monkey pussy show again; this time she had seven penises gathered round. Speaking once again about sex, it seems the Internet café here is very user friendly; that is to say, there are no filters to keep the porn out. The great thing is the marines here have done all the hard work, finding the best sites and book-marking them. So all I have to do is go check the favorites list and pick what I like. Some of the sites are pretty wild. I don't see the harm. These guys are way out here for a year, so what's the harm? I find it a welcome change from the Draconian restrictions placed on my computer back in Baghdad.

8 Nov 2000 hrs

Nothing unclassified happened today.

9 Nov 2200 hrs

Nothing unclassified happened today.

10 Nov 0700 hrs

I am back in Najaf from a short detour. Going to an Iraqi National Guard awards ceremony today. Sounds like a great target for a car bomber. I'll have to remember to find an escape route first thing.

2300 hrs

The ceremony was interesting to watch. The Iraqi soldiers don't have much of a sense of marching or rhythm right now. The drive through town was nice, once again sitting in the back of a seven-ton truck with our shit in the wind. It really isn't that bad; I prefer the open air to being locked inside an armored vehicle.

The rest of the day was a total waste of time. Some marine had written a song for his buddies who were killed in the cemetery. That part was cool; however, the fawning done by the chain of command was really embarrassing to the kid who wrote and performed the song. I know, because I asked him how he felt. Captain Dunkelberger was trying to get him on the morning news shows live in the states. Poor kid didn't want any of that attention. He just wrote the song to feel better about losing his friends.

11 Nov 2200 hrs

Today was so boring that I took a picture of a savage Iraqi grasshopper on my finger. It was really funny, because we were joking that it was wearing a suicide belt. Tomorrow I am going on a civil affairs patrol through the city. We will be stopping at various construction sites around the city. They have been doing tons of rebuilding in this city since the huge battle in the cemetery.

Well, I am off to bed soon. As for heading back to America, I have packed my bags over and over in my mind. Of course, I have also planned my funeral several times as well.

12 Nov 0700 hrs

Going on my patrol this morning. I like to listen to music before I go on a trip. I put a few Tootsie Rolls in my bag to throw out to the savage children that I see on the streets. Catch up with you in a few hours.

1315 hrs

Oh my, I had an amazing time in the city of Najaf today. We were right down by the shrine, which had al Sadr's people all fired up. I took tons and tons of photos. We dismounted the patrol and strolled through the heart of the old city. I saw so many Iraqis just living and going about their business: weavers, pot makers, and hawkers of all kinds. While were we were walking, we stopped to inspect a school that had been rebuilt. I could see the hole in the wall where American tanks had driven through. Now they were fixed, and everyone seemed happy with our presence. There were four of us, total, on the street. Our patrol slowly shadowed us without being overbearing. The public market seemed like a cross between what you see in an *Indiana Jones* movie and the public market in Seattle. It was fascinating to realize where I was and what I was seeing. There were fresh meat vendors with lamb hearts hanging in the window, and women selling fruits and vegetables off mats right in the middle of the road. Oh, the women; I had never seen so many Iraqi women in one place before. They were all wearing black robes, so I couldn't tell one from the other, but it was awesome. Just two months ago these streets were the scene of intense fighting. WOW!

2050 hrs

I convoyed back from FOB Hotel to FOB Duke, which is where I was a couple of weeks ago. I am awaiting a helicopter ride for transport back to either Camp Victory or the Green Zone. At this point, I would rather go back to base, sleep, re-fit, and leave again. I am a little tired from my adventures, classified and otherwise.

I am planning on making a third trip back to Fallujah. I want to lose my teammates. Traveling with others in a war zone is just like listening to people back in the states: "I'm tired, cold, hungry, lazy…" Whatever. When I travel with me, I listen to just me. This trip has been fun. Honestly, I ended up places doing things that seemed impossible a few months ago. Here's to a safe helicopter ride to wherever I end up tonight.

14 Nov 0330 hrs

The pilots dropped us off at my usual LZ here at Camp Victory. When we were flying into the city from the west, some pagan fired an RPG right at the front of out helicopter. This bird was an old marine CH-47, big and slow. The RPG passed along the left side and out into the darkness behind the tail, where it exploded. I was watching from my favorite seat. I was simply too tired to care. My guardian angel must be working overtime.

15 Nov 1100 hrs

I am in my tent. Four mortar rounds just landed in the compound, shaking my entire tent. The fucking terrorists have managed to kill a few people this way. I had yesterday completely off for recovery, plus I slept in again today. I have a terrific head cold again today. I didn't realize just how worn down I had become.

There were some places I went over the last few weeks and things I did that I can't write about here. I hope you understand. Fucking regulations.

2330 hrs

I am watching *The Simpsons* on DVD right now and nursing my sore throat. Trying to leave for a return trip tomorrow; one day in and out.

16 Nov 2300 hrs

Nothing official happened today.

17 Nov 2200 hrs

I got a serious ass-chewing from my sergeant major today. At least they know I am alive. I really enjoy getting yelled at by people who know I am smarter than them. I wrote some things down on paper about Captain Dunkelberger and his shortcomings on our most recent trip, so the sergeant major got his dander all up.

18 Nov 0900 hrs

I had a dream last night that I was at a whorehouse; John Kerry and Ted Kennedy were there as well. I asked John, "What are you doing here?" He said, "Leave me alone, I'm not running for president anymore." I looked at Kennedy; he said, "Hey, I am just here for the booze." My friends back in the states don't believe me when I tell them about the crazy dreams I have here. Usually it is just childhood memories that comfort me here. I did have another dream that I was traveling with Nancy Reagan. We stopped in Wyoming to do some shopping during a rodeo. Talk about wild dreams.

19 Nov 1115 hrs

In the military we use the twenty-four-hour system of time to avoid confusion between A.M. and P.M. for all times. Yesterday, Sergeant First Class Morrison told Sergeant Pippin to tell me to pick up some journalists at the helipad at 8:30. Since no one said 2030 hrs, I assumed it meant 0830 hrs the next day. I was relaxing in my tent when Sergeant First Class Morrison called me on my cell phone around 2130. In her smart-ass style of leadership she asks me, "When are supposed to pick people up?" I tell her tomorrow morning. She replies, "Fucking forget it. You were supposed to pick them up an hour ago." Then she hung up the phone. Great people skills! That is why we use the twenty-four-hour system, for just such instances. Tonight it was just picking someone up. Another day it could be important battle plans.

I had a terrible nightmare the other night. I was so afraid. It was one of those instances where you wake up and are still afraid, even though you know that you are awake and safe. Here is the dream: I was watching the entire universe spinning around on a device resembling a spectrograph. So I am watching this happen, then I realize that the universe is turning inside out. I realize that if this happens, everything that exists will cease to exist. I was terrified. Because I was watching the universe from on high, it shows I have achieved recognition of the problems that exist in the universe. I know that the violence here and around the world contributed to this nightmare. The fact that I recognize this should help in elevating my level of consciousness. This is something I will have to give lots more thought. I called my friend and college professor, Dr. Keith Quincy, to speak about my dream. He has a vast knowledge of philosophy and such. He was very interested in my dream and its interpretation.

20 Nov 1200 hrs

Last night I called Condoleezza Rice at the National Security Agency. I called to congratulate her on being selected for Secretary of State. It is nice to call people and have them recognize your name when asked for it. I can't relate the contents of the conversation; I'm sure it is privileged information.

I have to film a memorial service this afternoon. This will be the first one for a soldier I knew personally.

2200 hrs

The service was very hard for me to attend. I think filming it made it easier, because I had something to do. The soldier who was killed was Sergeant Dima. He was from Romania. I had met him when I was getting to know the soldiers who were becoming citizens a couple of months ago. I remember doing his interview and asking him what it was like to become a citizen. Being a soldier at a funeral of another soldier is very hard for me. It could easily be someone closer, or me. All soldiers seem to think like that at a wartime funeral. It is very easy to let your imagination run away with you.

21 Nov 2345 hrs

Lots of rockets were fired at us tonight. My friends and I were watching the Colts play the Bears when we heard them. Colonel Harrington and I ran outside to see for ourselves. Some of the rockets were bursting in the air, which causes shrapnel to be spread over a wide area. Later, when I returned to the office, there were some more, followed by one lonely dog yipping in the night. Got a great email from my friend Gail, back home in Washington. She asked lots of questions about how I feel being over here and if I have changed. Very thought-provoking inquiries. Thanks, Gail.

Well, I am off to bed. Here's hoping a rocket doesn't hit my tent. You people in America have it so easy, for now. Wait till the enemy comes.

22 Nov 1230 hrs

It seems everyone I know made it through the night, which is very good indeed. In answer to Gail's questions, I have changed quite a bit. On the outside, I am still happy and carefree, no matter what I encounter or see, personally or professionally. On the inside, the rage that I felt on September 11 has been molded into seething hatred for the terrorists as well as those who stand by and do nothing. Europeans, pacifists, and non-fighting Muslims have an obligation to stand against these enemies of peace, yet they do nothing.

23 Nov 2330 hrs

Lots of outgoing artillery last night into targets in the heart of the city. It was a nice change of pace. Usually, the command here just sits back and takes punch after punch on the chin. The best defense is a good offense! I really got into the big guns from my time in Fallujah. In other news, I've been running every night lately. I still have a hard time coming to grips with jogging in Iraq. Back home I would always jog or rollerblade to relax and unwind. Here, it is the same thing, except I am here in Southwest Asia. When I run at night and look up at the stars, I could be anywhere. In the daytime, I know I am in Iraq because of all the soldier stuff I have to wear. But at night, with a t-shirt and sneakers, I could be anywhere but here...

24 Nov 2240 hrs

Today I cried. I just sat down and let it out. The trigger was an email I got from my brother. He said he was headed out to our parents' house to start the holiday cooking for Thanksgiving. He said he would have a big turkey sandwich for me. All of the pain and suffering I have seen over here, yet it was thoughts of home that finally broke me down. My family isn't that close, but it would be nice to sit around the table and let my parents blame me personally for the successes of the Republican Party this year; to consume prodigious amounts of alcohol while my wife runs interference with my sister, her husband, and me. Which brings me to the real spirit of Thanksgiving: I am thankful to be alive today. I am also thankful to bring freedom to so many people who never knew it in their entire lifetime.

25 Nov 0900 hrs

Happy Thanksgiving. No shelling occurred last night; I was very surprised. These pagans keep track of important dates in America, so I know they won't want to miss today. I just spoke to my brother on the phone. The connection wasn't good, so I will call back in a few hours. I also called a man I met at the airport in Baltimore on the way here. His name is Richard. We had a very pleasant conversation the day we met in the airport. I have sent him occasional emails telling him how I've been doing. I firmly believe that people pay much more attention when they know someone personally who is here in Iraq, or anywhere, for that matter.

I officially have the day off, but I will go in to the office anyway. I have to work the phone and get away from here. I am getting that edgy, cooped up feeling. At lunchtime tomorrow I am supposed to accompany my foreign friends to gather food from the mess hall to take back to our building: "Operation Turkey Grab."

1836 hrs

This morning I had to follow three senators around Baghdad who were here on a fact finding mission. This was a real treat for me, as I am a total political junkie. The senators visiting were Senator Kyl from Arizona, Senator Chambliss from Georgia, and Senator Nelson from Nebraska. It was awfully nice of them to take time away from their families over the holidays to come and visit the troops here in Iraq. During the visit, we all watched Iraqi commandos doing urban assault training. The scenario was a hostage rescue. It involved a ground and air insertion from hovering helicopters. It was very high speed stuff. Afterward, Senator Chambliss said a few words to the Iraqis about how brave they are to try to secure their own country.

When I returned for lunch, around 1300 hrs, my friends were already eating. I had missed the rendezvous time for the lunchtime operation. Well, it didn't stop me from digging right in. I had homemade gumbo, courtesy of Specialist Franks, and all the turkey and fixins from the mess hall. Now, after all this eating, I am heading out for my evening run.

2100 hrs

Just spoke to my wife back in Texas. She is sad because she is alone on this holiday. We have friends there who she could go and be with, yet she is choosing not to go. I can't make her, so that is all right, I guess. The hardest part of being here is being away from those I love; it is not the bombs, bullets, or beheadings.

I am sitting in front of the TV watching the Colts and the Lions play. Amy just said it is only the Colts that are playing; the Lions are only watching.

2300 hrs

The Ukrainian colonel brought in a fifth of Johnny Walker Red label for us all to have. Of course, I am not allowed alcohol as a member of the U.S. Forces here. So I may or may not have some. Hey, I am a compulsive liar. Which is it? The toasting is always the best when among these friends from different nations. It is getting late, and I still have friends to call back home.

26 Nov 2100 hrs

My command has gone and done it now. They are really trying to help me over the edge by giving me that last little push.

On an enjoyable note, I did film a concert at the palace today. What a contrast to where I have been in the last few weeks: in Fallujah firing cannons, cruising the streets in Najaf, and now a Thanksgiving concert by an all-male coalition choir group. It features all branches and ranks. I didn't particularly enjoy the event, but I filmed it so that those who participated can have a copy of the news story I put together. I move around and collect different shots. When things like this are over, people expect a copy of the whole thing. Hey, I am a newsman, not your camera bitch wife back home, buddy.

I have been reading my journal entries from the beginning. I must say, some are to die for funny, while others have been more enlightening than amusing. I am very happy that I stuck it out and continued to write every day. Many people I've spoken to intended to keep a journal, but they just couldn't keep up with it, I guess.

27 Nov 1000 hrs

This morning someone pointed out something funny in the newspaper that the military publishes here in Iraq. One of the reporter's names is B.J. Weiner. That is funny shit! Everyone in the office wanted to call the paper as a prank phone call, but no one had the balls to do it. Of course, I volunteered to do it. So I called, cool as ice, and asked for Mr. B.J. Weiner, if you please. They hung up the phone. When we called back, they said it was a bad connection on the phone. Regardless, it was nice to execute a prank call in a war zone.

2200 hrs

I learned something very interesting about two of my friends here in Iraq. They are seeing each other romantically. I missed all the signs, because I'm caught up in my own existence much of the time. Of course, in a living situation like this, gossip is a major pastime. Not so much for me; I'm busy doing things all the time, including work, so I haven't had much time for gossip. I won't write down their names, because you never know who may come along down the road and find what you have written. I don't know if this is a war romance or something that will last. The man is not an American soldier, while the girl is, so we shall see if it lasts after he departs and she goes home as well.

28 Nov 0800 hrs

Was supposed to meet with Colonel Howard last night at 2100 hrs to show him my D9 dozer footage. I went to his office, but he never showed up. Oh well, I'm still getting paid. I'm supposed to play flag football today, down at the motor pool. We have an organized flag football league here, but I have a meeting with our public relations firm at the same time. Such is war, interfering with my flag football plans. On the subject of the firm, who hires a public relations firm to help in a war? Some things I just don't understand, and maybe that is for the best.

We haven't been attacked here for the last three nights in a row, and that is a pleasant feeling.

1815 hrs

Many times I have found that I have thoughts or feelings that I cannot write down, or in essence, discuss with myself. Part of it results from my actions—either official or unofficial—which can't be discussed outside the military establishment. Sometimes these events are exciting and dangerous, while others are loathsome and painful. I can't explain the emotional burden that is placed upon you when you have documents or briefings that are secret and in your possession, or having to send emails on a secret, secure server. What a world we live in.

29 Nov 2330 hrs

We had a going away party tonight for our Italian friends, specifically Brigadier General De Pascale. The American Forces chief of staff gave everyone permission to drink champagne in honor of this event. Yippee, real sweet booze! Fortunately, there was much more to drink than there were people to drink it. *Happy days are here again, happy days.* My boss, Lieutenant Colonel Baggio, was at this party as well. We were standing around talking and he said, "Hey, Kiver, can I get you a beer?" "Sure," I replied. Lieutenant O'Neil came walking by. I grabbed her by the arm and said, "Watch this." Sure enough, Lieutenant Colonel Baggio returned and gave me a beer in front of her. It was so funny that my boss would get a beer for me like that. Maybe civilians don't see the humor, but in the military, it was a gut busting moment.

30 Nov 0830 hrs

I may need some hair of the dog that bit me. Last night was tons of fun. The guest list for the party was top heavy with lots of brass, which is typical for parties in the military. I was sitting at a table eating with four colonels: one from the marines is Colonel Harrington, whom I know well; another was Colonel Little, U.S. Army, whom I see around occasionally; and the other two were unknown to me. One of them asked Colonel Little who I was. Colonel Little replied, "That is the broadcast journalist, Kiver. He's funny as hell, and good people." That made me feel good about me!

1600 hrs

More stories from the party. Two of my friends who are dating each other had the funniest fight in the kitchen last night. The girl kept opening bottles of champagne and drinking them with all of us. The man came in and was upset because the general was still in the building, and he thought we would get in trouble, even though we had permission to drink on this night. He was screaming at her, "I swear to God, if you don't put the bottle down, I'm going to kick your ass!" However, she held her ground, refusing to budge. She reminded me of an angry drunk bulldog that was backed into a corner.

Today I spoke with Colonel Howard, USMC, about production of my bull dozer video as well as getting back to Fallujah for more interviews with key engineers in the Marine Corps. Right now I am sitting in the Ford Explorer, waiting to pick up some Iraqi laborer who can fix the satellite dish that is busted on the roof of the palace. These people can be shifty if you don't keep an eye on them all the time.

Spoke to my wife today. She's upset about our anniversary. We exchanged cards, but she wanted more. I don't know what else I could have done. I'm way over here in Iraq. What can I do? The day was very important to me. All of my friends knew that it was my anniversary and that it meant a lot to me. Everyone except my wife! Which makes it my fault again…?

1 Dec 1130 hrs

I have not been this mad ever in my life. A producer from Fox contacted me about being on a national talk radio program back in America. He received my information from Oliver North, whom I had met here in Baghdad. I forwarded the request to my bosses in the palace. This morning they said "No." I know that it didn't go to the colonel's desk; it stopped with Sergeant First Class Mor— and the sergeant major. I am furious! This is an incredible opportunity for the army, our public affairs mission here, as well as me as an army journalist. Imagine, national radio, and perhaps even on a weekly basis. Did you know that the army hired a civilian public relations firm? They say it is because the firm can do things in the community that we cannot because of regulations and stuff. Bullshit! The palace rangers are failing every day to convince the rest of the world that what is going on here is right. If we can't do that well at home, how can we convince the people being blown up here every day that the cause is just? It's just like I've always said: it is like trying to scream over a freight train. This afternoon I will be out hunting car bombers on the highway outside the base, as I said last night. I am looking forward to it. Anything to take my mind off of these frustrations. At this point, I would rather be killed in a blaze of glory than deal with these aggravations. No, I'm not being dramatic. I am so fucking through with these headless chickens I work worth. I went outside the trailer where I work and picked up a two-by-four and broke it by striking a pile of sandbags. Talk about adrenaline surge. These bastards in the palace wouldn't know a public relations coup if it bit them in their camel toe.

2000 hrs

Went out to the guard towers on the airport road this afternoon. Unfortunately, nothing happened. The company commander told me they will set up a nightshift that I can hang out with the whole time. That is when things happen mostly. I am lying in my tent, which is about a half mile from the road, listening to gunfire and explosions, and I want to take pictures of that up close. I must be a loony. The airport road is called Route Irish by the military. When I first got here, we took trips in Ford Explorers down to the Green Zone, downtown on that road. All that was necessary were two vehicles and four soldiers with rifles. I can't believe this, but those were the good ol' days. Now it is armor and four vehicles; no more taking the SUVs for a spin through downtown Baghdad.

2 Dec 0913 hrs

I'm very tired. I don't like being tired here. It makes me feel like I am slow and sluggish. I want to remain alert all the time, being ready to jump behind a building when a rocket or mortar comes in. The reason I am tired is because my tent filled up yesterday with a bunch of rookies from the states. I didn't get any sleep at all. I went from having no roommates to having seven. It will be fine; I just have to get used to it.

People back home always ask, "How do you deal with getting shelled, or the possibility that it could happen at any time?" The sad thing is you get used to it. As I related on numerous occasions, they just land, and hopefully you're not close to it. The other day there was a really loud explosion outside our office. I said to my buddy, "If we were back home, I would run outside to see what the hell that was." But because it's Iraq, you just don't worry about things you can't control. When it's your time, that's just it. This brings up an interesting question that I have to answer for myself. Am I better off because I am used to the attacks? Or have I lost innocence of youth that can never be regained? If wisdom comes with experience, then I am as wise as they come.

Well, I'm going to take a nap now. When my coworkers start making sense, I am way too tired.

2230 hrs

Went to dinner tonight with my Italian friends, who are leaving tomorrow afternoon. Also with us was the American girl who has been seeing my buddy, as I've told you before. Ah, the perils of love in a war zone. She has been having separation anxiety all week long. I don't think it will be a pretty sight tomorrow.

Yesterday our battalion sergeant major yelled at the entire formation, telling us how much danger we were in, as one soldier was receiving a Purple Heart that morning. No shit, Sherlock! Like I don't hear the rockets and the car bombs? I may put on a good show, but I realize the dangers. He really made an ass out of himself, saying things like, "You are not safe here; you are secure, but you are not safe." Thanks, genius, I think I'll name my first child after you: Dumb ass.

3 December 0100 hrs

Yes, I'm still up. I'm waiting till I'm really tired to go back to my tent. Just heard a car bomb go off out on Route Irish. A second later, the AH-Apache attack helicopters came flying by to check out the scene. Just another dead Arab extremist and some wounded soldiers, I'm sure. Fucking pagans! (People against goodness and normalcy.)

1517 hrs

Saw my Italian friends off on their way to the airfield. Three of them left because their tours were up. An American marine who works in the same building was sitting behind me lamenting about people leaving. I can't remember his exact words, but they seemed to be making the point that you make good friends, and then they are gone from your life. He is leaving in about ten days to return to America as well. I signed his Marine Corps flag for him. I wrote, "Sir, thanks for pouring, Senator Kiver." He is a good guy, this marine. So Roberto is gone, as well as Antonio and Brigadier General De Pascale. Their replacements are here, and I will continue to hang out at the building in the evenings as much as possible to make them feel welcome, to make new friends to replace the ones I have lost. Fortunately, there are still enlisted friends there as well.

Tomorrow I will be flying down south to witness the completion of a major highway project linking North and South here in Iraq. I love flying in helicopters!

This morning there were four car bombings, one right after the other, out along the highway. I heard them from my tent along with the gunfire. Then, this afternoon, I read about the attacks on the Internet. It's like seeing yourself on TV; very surreal that you are always right where the news is happening. Fortunately, it was Arab on Arab violence; bad for us, but bad for terrorists as well. How can you do that to your own people just because they want freedom? The police and soldiers want to make this country prosper. The terrorists want the Stone Age to return. The choice seems clear enough to me!

4 Dec 0800 hrs

There was a massive explosion last night—surely it was a rocket attack—and I'm headed over to the Joint Operations center to get the facts. I have to be at the LZ in fifty-eight minutes to catch my helicopter ride for the day. Total cost: zero dollars. Thanks, John Q taxpayer.

Later …

0915 hrs

So, I am at LZ Griffin, waiting on (you guessed it) my helicopter!

2000 hrs

A few days ago, my friend Gail asked me in an email what a typical day was like for me here in Iraq. Here goes. I woke up this morning, went for a run, showered and shaved, and experienced the above related events. When the helicopter landed, I took the front middle seat, which allows me to see the pilots, the front window, and the two door gunners. It is the best seat in the bird! I was lucky, as both helicopters were full. We flew for about thirty minutes and had to stop at some marine forward operating base for jet fuel—JP8, for those who wish to know. Pay attention to the fueling stop, it comes into play later. After getting gas, we flew for another forty minutes, then we started making corkscrew circles round and round. This is where if you look out one side of the helicopter you see ground, the other side you see sky. If you look out the front, it appears as if your TV has fallen on its side. I looked at the copilot. He was looking at a map. Are you serious? We were lost! They had missed the rendezvous point! So we turned around and flew for another ten minutes, which should alert you to the fact that we missed the LZ by more than a little bit! Anyhow, we saw the purple smoke, which means "land here." It was just a lonely stretch of highway, with lots of people and vehicles milling about. The event today was a joining of the two highway ends, as completed by Iraqis and engineers from the Utah National Guard. They proceeded to bang a golden spike into the highway as historical significance. Look up Promontory Point 1868 if you want to know the meaning. This only took a few minutes. Instead of getting back on the helicopters, I jumped in a Humvee convoy to take me to Talill Airbase, which is where the choppers were headed anyway with all the generals and stuff. Oh, of course I took video and digital images of the ceremony. All kidding aside, the project is very important for troop safety in Iraq. Fully, twenty-five percent of U.S. deaths here are attributed to vehicle accidents; twenty-five percent, which amounts to about three hundred some boys right now.

So we made it to base. Some of the generals wanted to go to the ziggurat! Yeah! I love this place. It is like an *Indiana Jones* amusement park, as I have said before. We screwed around out there for a while; I bought some things at the gift shop. No, I am not kidding. Drove back to the airfield; this time the choppers were already there. Thank God for small favors. We jumped on, and were off. My seat this time was second row, facing the back left side, only one window to look out. Not a good seat. Again, we had to stop for fuel; this is where I told you to pay attention. They make you get off while they are fueling, just in case there is some sort of accident. These are hot stops with the engines running. My coworker decided she would light a cigarette to try to blow us all up. I was all over her before she took the first puff. What a fucking moron! Thirty years old and she is going to smoke next to jet fuel. Another Darwin award, if you please. Back on the helicopters and home to Baghdad. I yelled at her in the office. She refused to accept that what she had done was wrong. So I'll bring that up at the staff meeting in the morning. This brings me to where I am now, on the computer. How did you like my day, Gail? Well, I'm going to run along now.

5 Dec 2030 hrs

One of the rookies in my tent asked me this morning if I heard any explosions last night. I said, "Nope, didn't wake me up at all." With a worried expression he asked me how to tell if they were incoming or outgoing. I just smiled and said, "Ask my gorilla, he will tell you." My stuffed gorilla, that is; I sleep with him every night. If I were at home, I would hold my wife close, but that isn't happening for another couple of months. I had a dream the other night that I was home with my wife. I just sat on her lap and cried. I still dream of home every night, even if sometimes they are not good. I have a meeting at 0900 hrs tomorrow with a lieutenant to get out on a guard tower along the highway for a shift. I am really looking forward to getting on the tower. Just like in *A Few Good Men*, I eat breakfast across from five million Iraqis who have no training but would like to kill me.

Talked to my father on the phone today. He is a geologist by trade, so I was telling him about my latest trip down to Ur. You remember; he teaches at my university. It made things easier, because most of the professors already knew who I was. I had so much fun at college; I really miss the personal interaction. When I did my master's program online, it was so lonely, not being in a classroom. I also spoke to my sister and her husband on the phone today as well. Not much to talk about; we don't really like one another. I just called to say hi, is all.

Just received a warning order today that I may be headed down to Basra in a couple of weeks. I have wanted to get down there for sometime, as it is very near the Persian Gulf, and a perfect place to swim!

I miss my Italian buddies, but their replacements seem cool enough, so I have still been hanging out in their building. In fact, tonight I was mixing some beverages in the kitchen when a marine friend of mine came in. He picked up a glass that had a small amount of beverage that had been given to me by a colonel from the country of Moldova. My friend asked, "Can I try this?" "Sure, knock yourself out," I replied. He took a swig, and couldn't speak. His mouth and throat had been burned by the act of consumption. Yet another lesson of why you don't play around with jet fuel. It was so funny to see him gasping! I am about ready to go for a run around the lake. It is dark and chilly, but peaceful all the same. I don't know if I'll ever fathom taking a jog in a war zone such as this. Maybe some night at home I'll wake up screaming in a cold sweat.

2215 hrs

I just returned from my run, and logged on to the *Seattle Times* website to read the news from my home state. There was an article about a guardsman from the unit I used to be in, who was terribly wounded in Iraq. His Humvee was blown up by a shell buried in the road. His gunner was killed, while the other soldier escaped with no injuries. The road where it happened is a road I have been down, just outside LSA Anaconda, fifty miles north of Baghdad. I feel guilty right now. Almost ten thousand Americans have been wounded, with around thirteen hundred killed. Why not me? Who decides who gets hit and who doesn't? I have been shot at; I have been in helicopters that have been shot at. Remember the ride home from Anaconda the night they were firing at my helicopter? I was so tired that I didn't care if it was the end. What sort of protection surrounds me? I have flown around five hundred flight hours and driven thousands of kilometers in this savage land, yet only a few bruises and scratches. I'm not out for glory; I just want to know I did everything I could. Perhaps I have "Sam" to thank; after all, I did purchase and read his autobiography. I don't want to push my luck either. I just want to do what I'm supposed to do. I gave an interview to the local television station back in Texas before I left. My wife was with me when they asked, "What are your goals in Iraq?" I replied, "Coming home with all my fingers and toes." I need sleep, or booze—maybe both. But I am only allowed one. Kiver has left the building.

6 Dec 2000 hrs

Mortar in the courtyard in a truck; I went to see the commander.

7 Dec 2330 hrs

Just came back in from the base perimeter. There are towers all along the walls at our base. I decided to go out there and interview some of the guys who help keep us safe here at Camp Victory. These particular soldiers are National Guardsmen from my home state. The shift that I was on is 1700 to 0100 hrs. They told me that they've been on the shift for the last nine months, seven days a week. Their morale was very good considering that they get shot at frequently. Nothing of consequence happened during my time with them. It was a great experience for me, though, to see how shift workers cope with the requirements of their jobs. From my vantage point, I was able to see convoys and patrols driving up and down the road. The highway, as you may remember, is the airport road, as they call it. I paused for a moment, looking at the soldiers through my night vision goggles, realizing that before the night was through, there was a good chance that some of them could be hurt or killed. But such is your duty over here. While hanging out in the tower, I called my mom and dad on the cell phone to tell them where I was. Imagine calling home from a place like that. Well, I did it in Fallujah, why not from a guard tower as well. My mother told me that some girl from high school had called about my ten-year reunion next year.

She gave me the number so I could call. When I got this girl on the phone, I told her where I was calling from. She told me our high school wasn't being supportive in her quest to bring everyone together. I replied, "Those fuckers." She didn't like my language at all. I told her I'm in a war zone, I talk how I want! She thanked me for my service and said she would email the information to me about the reunion.

Back to guard duty. Sitting up in the tower really gave me a new perspective on the explosions and gunfire I hear all the time from my tent. These are real people out there protecting the rest of us while we go about our business. These soldiers and I really got to know each other in the few short hours we spent together. I'm glad I took the opportunity to go out there. You just assume when you are on a U.S. base that you will be safe no matter what. But look at what happened in Saudi Arabia: the American Consulate was stormed and people were killed. As one of the soldiers said, "I am the first line of defense if someone wants to come over this wall." I'm glad he's out there protecting me while I am writing about it here in my office. Everyone does their part over here without much complaint, and for that I am appreciative, even more so with this being the anniversary of Pearl Harbor Day.

8 Dec 1200 hrs

Something very funny happened to me just now. I was handing out Christmas cards to the troops, which had been delivered to me by two great Americans back home: Kimberly in Pennsylvania and Cynthia in Kentucky. I work and socialize regularly with foreign members of the coalition. So I gave some cards to an Italian major and a Ukrainian colonel. The colonel took the card and in a thick Russian accent said, "In old Soviet Union, school children would write letters to Soviet soldiers in the army. So now that Americans do it, they must be adopting old

Soviet program." To which I replied, "In America, people write letters because they want to, not because they are told to." He continued to be very adamant about the letter writing program. But seriously, I like the colonel. He is a very gregarious and physically jolly fellow. Perhaps I should take his picture.

9 Dec 1430 hrs

Just rotated all of my ammunition for my M-16. Since the magazines are spring loaded, you cannot leave the ammo in too long or it will damage the springs. So every few days I take it out, let the springs recover, if you will, then fill them up again.

Staff Sergeant Mattox related a really funny story today. It seems this morning he was in the bathroom, which is a conex box setup, where he was taking a leak. The Filipino cleaning ladies came in and started slapping the floor with the hot mops while he was there hanging out, as it were. He said he almost asked the ladies if they would give him a good cleaning. Ha ha! That's good stuff, Staff Sergeant Mattox.

2230 hrs

Just had a nice conversation with my father on the phone. My parents are enjoying the Christmas season back home in Washington. We talked about what they have been up to and stuff. My mom has been printing out the digital photos I send to them via email to make a scrapbook of my time in Iraq. My dad and I spoke about how some days over here are good, so much that I don't think I would ever want to leave. Others days are bad and I wish I could go home. Now, those days have been few and far between, but they do happen. I'm sure Michael Moore or someone would like to take my words out of context and say that I don't want to be here, but that is not the case. I 'm happy to be here and do my part in this historic undertaking in Iraq. We freed millions of people here—people who now have access to two hundred newspapers to read. They are free to worship as they please—even free to make fun of their leaders, if they want.

We had Christmas tree lighting in the palace this evening. It did make me sad, but on the other hand, I will one day be able to say that I spent Christmas in Baghdad one year when I was younger. The ceremony was nice; it featured an all-men's choir group that was formed here at Camp Victory. It is hard to see these reminders of home, yet realize that you are not there to be with your loved ones. Yet it is our presence here that makes it safer for those at home. I'm glad terrorists come to Iraq to try to kill me; at least they aren't going to America to do the same thing.

My wife will be going home for the holidays to visit our families. She has been having a very difficult time as of late. I don't want to write a lot about it. Her suffering wears on me very much. I don't know if I could be here without her support. Yet she needs my support so much as well. I don't empathize well at all. It is hard for me to equate getting shot at with being lonely.

10 Dec 1731 hrs

Time to start thinking about hitting the road again. Today I had to help officers with very simple tasks, which is funny and sad at the same time. First, I took a DVD over to Brigadier General Pullhman, and had to sit there while they made sure there was sound on it. One of the soldiers appeared to be being a little friendly toward me. She was skinny, with straight lines for a body, except her teeth, which were all crooked. Of course, I blew her off, regardless of what she looked like. After that I had to go up to the palace and help a lieutenant colonel play a videotape and record it onto a DVD at the same time. This involved pushing play on the VCR, then pushing record on the DVD player. I know

I have a master's degree, but seriously, everywhere I look I see dumb people.

My wife is flying back home today to be with her loved ones. I told her to be vigilant for terrorists on the flight. They are out there waiting and watching; I'm sure of it. I don't need my government to tell me that. I'm seeing it here firsthand.

The weather here is very pleasant for December; it is just like fall in the Pacific Northwest. A couple of guys moved out of my tent today. The camp is getting very crowded, as units are moving in and out for this next rotation. It is sad seeing people go that I have become accustomed to seeing. But I know they are going home to their families, just like I will. Another benefit of the rotation is new people are coming in. I went to lunch today with an Italian warrant officer who is new here, so we had a pleasant conversation. Tomorrow he is cooking dinner for all of us. Sometimes it feels like a vacation over here. We haven't gotten shelled lately, which makes things seem a little better. I know as soon as I give complacency a chance, they will strike again. I'm going to go out to a different guard tower in the next couple of nights.

I had another good conversation with my father on the phone again last night. We were speaking about war and the effects of being over here. My father was in the Coast Guard for ten years when he was younger. So we kinda have that in common. Well, I'm going to go grab my dirty uniform and wash it while I go for a run around the lake.

2100 hrs

I'm listening to the song "Have You Forgotten?" by Darryl Worley. It's a country music song that was written for the war in

Afghanistan. I don't get caught up in where the war is physically. This conflict is worldwide. Liberal or conservative, when the terrorists blow your plane up, will they stop to ask you who you voted for?

Saw the news today, with some soldier complaining about a lack of armored vehicles. Every vehicle that I have been in on the roads in Iraq had some sort or armor. Some were factory-made top quality steel doors with ballistic glass. These are nice rides, with everything fitting snug and tight. Others were homemade welded steel. These have openings all over, where you could be shot or bombed. Still, other times I stood in the back of a Humvee with my camera on a monopod so I could get the footage I needed, with no thought of getting shot. Every time I went out and did my mission, I did so without complaining about where I had to sit. It is monkey see, monkey do. War is risky; armor won't save your life every time. Soldiers in tanks and Bradleys have been killed simply by the shockwave that goes through the vehicle. It literally scrambles your brain, because the energy has no way to escape.

Soldiers are right to question their leaders in appropriate forums. Soldiers also have the right to shut the hell up and drive on with the mission. I do it every day. I disagree with tons of stuff that my bosses come up with, but I do it anyway. This armor issue was such a load of shit. It never should have been allowed to grow as large as it did.

11 Dec 0033 hrs

I'm still awake listening to these tribute songs for 9-11 that several singers recorded. Just now writing, I realized it is 12-11; I don't know why. It just hit me hard today that I'm part of the worldwide conflict. I am so hopeful for the country of Iraq and its people. I have to keep the positive attitude in order to keep going. Tonight I was thinking that I'm afraid to go home, knowing I'll be leaving people I know behind. Luckily, I have more than a month to come to grasp with the fact that I'll be leaving. Sometimes it feels like I've been here forever, yet I've only been here around four months.

2235 hrs

I just heard myself say something strange at dinner tonight. I was dining in Building 35 with the coalition partners, when I said, "If I wasn't married, I would stay in Iraq until the last American soldier leaves." Everyone looked at me like I was crazy! I think I meant it though. I am very comfortable here, even amid the violence and craziness. Just this morning three rockets landed in the trailer village where many soldiers live. I heard them fly over my tent just before impact. It is as much of a fact of life here as drunk driving is in the states during the holiday season. Odds are you are going to see it sometime. I was on the phone earlier with a friend back home. We kept getting interrupted by armored vehicles and helicopters whirling by. "Boy, it's like you live in a *Rambo* movie," she screamed in the phone.

12 December 1635 hrs

Lots of incoming rounds today. I mean, all day long it seems they have been shelling us. I was up at the north end of the base when four rounds came in. I was walking through the parking lot when they exploded. Lots of people were around and didn't even seem to notice. The shopping opportunities are plentiful here in Baghdad. We have AAFES, which stands for Army Air Force Exchange Service. It is like a big department store where you can buy things you need. There are also lots of Iraqi vendors who operate here on base as well. There is a huge market for pirated DVDs. Brand new, first-run movies pirated in theaters are sold here for two dollars a piece. I don't think it is right to steal movies like that, but who am I? Regardless, the Iraqis who sell them make tons of money. It doesn't matter where you go in Iraq; these profiteers are everywhere. There is a going away party tonight for someone who I don't even know, but luckily I have other things to do. I will enjoy not being up at the palace for a change. I'm going to try to get out on a different guard tower this week to continue my story about these brave guys who protect the rest of us from the savages.

13 December 2353 hrs

Today, today, today. Sometimes they all seem to run into the next one. Earlier I was hunting for marines here at Camp Victory. I needed to get some short interviews from them for the Toys for Tots campaign back in Texas. There are not many marines at this base, so I went looking for the ones I actually knew by name. I interviewed one colonel who says he has done lots of work for Toy for Tots during his career. This marine is Colonel Reynolds. He was Colonel Harrington's replacement. I really miss that old razorback.

Our camp is becoming very crowded these days: new units coming in while old ones are moving out, so there is an overlap when everyone is here at the same time. The mess hall is very crowded, as is my tent right now, although two more guys moved out today; however, I'm sure that will be short-lived. On the incoming fire front, it was very quiet today. As we get closer to the elections in Iraq, I am sure it will become like the Tet offensive. The fire we take has mostly been, well, I don't want to say harassment, because people have gotten killed. But it comes and goes. Our artillery, on the other hand, could flatten a thousand-meter-grid square in a matter of a few minutes, if we chose to do so.

I really feel for the National Guard soldiers I see. Many of them look so glassy eyed, like they have no idea how they got here. But hell, they signed a contract. The positive side is that no more than thirty percent of our reserve forces are here at any one time. So everyone will get their chance to come and spend some time in Iraq. These facts that I put out might confuse those who only listen to John Kerry, or CNN. Sorry about that, folks.

14 Dec 1900 hrs

Today we had an awesome USO show here in Baghdad. I had been to one other USO show, but it was in the states. So this was my first experience with an overseas show. To set the scene for you, there was a simple wooden stage of good size, built out of two-by-sixes and plywood. The parking lot, which was mostly gravel, contained around two thousand people: a good mix of U.S. and coalition troops, as well as Iraqi workers and third country nationals, who work here as well, but aren't from Iraq. Everyone had their digital/video cameras out for the occasion. One observation, this is certainly the most photographed war ever. A band made up of soldiers played for the opening act. Meanwhile, the crowd was buzzing because of who was supposed to appear: John Elway, Robin Williams, and Blake, whose last name I don't know. He played the ragin' Cajun coach in the movie *The Waterboy*. You know, the guy in overalls with the pierced nipples. Anyway, last but not least was some tits and ass named Leeann Tweeden from the *Best Damn Sports Show Period*. Milling about, I looked for someone I could interview. I spied three women in civilian clothes with U.S. contractor ID cards. I started asking them questions in an interview fashion before I identified myself as a journalist. One girl, named Pepper, said, "You are not getting our tent number from us." I told her to relax, that I was simply writing an article. After I gave them my business card, she realized I was just doing my job. Pepper is from Houston, Texas. The second girl, Jennifer, is from Austin, Texas. She never seemed as uptight about talking as Pepper did. Jennifer's nickname, which she volunteered, is Pippie. Pippie and Pepper—how annoying that could be, if you let it. Last was Katie. She was a tiny little thing, who said she was from Savannah, Georgia. She had the southern accent, but when I started pressing her about the Civil War, she backtracked and said she was originally from Southern California. These three girls became rather talkative after they realized I wasn't trying to score with them or anything. Any girl over here has to be wary. Together, these girls work for Kellogg Brown and Root (KBR), which is a subsidiary of Halliburton. Oh, the humanity! When cannons shot Brown and Root, for historical purposes, President Lyndon Johnson hitched his wagon to that company and got them lots of contracts during Vietnam, which is why they are so successful now. So don't go blaming Dick Cheney for the amount of money that company makes.

So these girls are over here making more money than most of the soldiers, but hey, this is a semi-free country here in Iraq. I talked to them about their jobs working in the motor pool, which mess halls they liked, and just general chitchat. It was nice to have a real conversation with people who don't have any connection to what I do. One thing Jennifer said that was really funny was about the recent Thanksgiving holiday. "We ate four kinds of meat that night." For less scrupulous girls, that would be very funny; however, my impression of her was that she was as pure as the driven show.

Overall, these three were very nice, and I'm glad they took the time to talk. Walking around I saw another female, an army soldier who was wearing makeup. Porno pink was the shade. She was really dolled up for being in uniform. Some girls come here for one thing, and some men oblige them in return. Enough of the crowd. John Elway came out on the stage and started talking about how proud he was to be an American. In the middle of his speech, two Black Hawk helicopters flew over at about sixty feet, drowning out his voice. It was awesome being at a USO show in a combat zone. After John was the next comedian, Blake. He was very, very funny, talking about being a redneck from Georgia and shit. The main event was Robin Williams; he put on a show for twenty minutes or so. He really hammered the armor issue that has been in the news lately. Of course, he also said, "Good morning, Baghdad!" Throughout all the performances, the T&A girl was giving us her two cents worth. I couldn't have cared less. Overall, the show was a huge success, with autograph signing and picture taking all around, for as many people as possible. When Robin was taking pictures with people, I cracked a one-liner about a girl crouching in front for her picture. She was looking at Robin instead of the camera. A security guard told her to turn around. I added, "Hey, turn around, before I hit it from the wrong end." Robin busted up laughing and even repeated it back to me. I was flattered I made Robin Williams laugh. Thanks to the USO and those who support it. From all us guys over here in harm's way, it is really a blessing to have an organization like this. If anyone reads this, please consider giving time or money to the USO. It makes a difference.

15 Dec 1700 hrs

Specialist Birmingham is complaining about having to take a physical fitness test two days from now. Everyone in the office will have to take a test that consists of pushups, sit-ups, and a two-mile run. She wanted more notice, because she hasn't been training. So would I, but hell, this is the army; do what you are told. Maybe if she hadn't *smoked* so much when she was younger (which she has admitted to on several occasions), she would remember that we are in the army, and also remember that you are not to smoke cigarettes on the flight line.

2300 hrs

My coworkers are all starting to ask about my journal writings. It seems they have noticed that I have continued writing in it all this time. Now they are concerned about what I may have written about them. Many of them are not even mentioned by name, as they aren't around me enough to get noticed. A really funny thing was when one person asked what I had written about them, when in actuality, they weren't in my journal at all.

I packed up two trunks today in preparation for putting them in a conex trailer, which will go home by ship the first of the year. In essence, I'm stripping down my living quarters to the bare minimum; you know, music, DVDs, non-water, magazines. Oh, I guess I should keep some clothes as well. Of course, it wouldn't be the army if they didn't provide a list of prohibited items that you can't ship or take home; for example, elephant parts, explosives, slugs, snails, or insects. Okay, here are some more; these are priceless: camel saddles, products from turtles, live animals, wild animals, birds, or parts thereof, alive or dead. This includes birds, reptiles, amphibians, mollusks, fish, or dead body, egg or other part. Now this is exactly how it was written and given to the soldiers. While the list is very long, here is the last one I will share: pet rocks! I am sure going to miss my pet rock, since I used it to kill and skin my first elephant, which I made into hunting utensils, which I used to then kill lots of turtles, birds, and mollusks. But what really kills me is that I can't bring a camel saddle home with me.

16 Dec 1300 hrs

I was walking to work this morning when I realized that we hadn't been shelled in a couple of days. When I was in the office, I remarked to my coworkers about it. Specialist Joyce said, "Hey, we just had one a few minutes ago, didn't you hear it?" I said, "Oh, come on; if it doesn't rattle the windows or my teeth, then it really shouldn't count." Specialist Birmingham, who doesn't want to take her fitness test tomorrow, claims to have had an accident on her bicycle this morning. Now I don't know if she did or not, but now she is not going to take the test. Feel free to look up the definition of *malingering* on your own. I just lay out the facts; I don't make accusations. I did, however, tell her that I have absolutely no respect for her based on her actions leading up to and including this latest incident, or lack thereof. Again, without pointing fingers, I simply can't believe that some people have so little integrity that they would make up absolute silliness.

I just realized that I haven't eaten in the mess hall in about a week. It just seems like such a waste of time for me right now. I'm still producing stories for my office. Meanwhile, Colonel Howard has me working on the dozer video. One of my tent mates is a serious snorer. This morning I came home to sleep around 0100 hrs. This dude was snoring something fierce. Since I wanted to sleep, I made lots of noise and turned on the light. This woke him up. Since he was awakened, I was able to fall asleep. My ten-man tent currently has three soldiers besides me. I prefer to live by myself. Well, I have my stuffed gorilla to keep me company. I know it may seem strange to have a stuffed animal, but it's all whimsical to me, so I will be taking gorilla home on the airplane.

I'm really looking forward to the elections and wish I could stay here longer to see them through. As it is, I am supposed to leave the very next day; that is, if the savages haven't blown up the entire country and themselves as well. I'm still just as much in favor of this war today as I was before I arrived. The facts are still coming to light about Saddam. Another mass grave with at least five hundred bodies was discovered just this week. Shh, not too loud; I don't want CNN to have to ignore what I am saying, so I'll keep it quiet. Fucking traitors!

1730 hrs

Well, I just shaved off all my hair! Sergeant First Class Morrison saw that my hair had been dyed red, so she told me it didn't look like a natural color. In the army you can have dyed hair if it looks good and your command likes you; however, since it appears I am the problem child, I don't have any currency to spend with them. Besides that, the III Corps sergeant major, Joe Gainey, was in our office when he said to me, "You, soldier, are just way out there." I think I was just insulted. Oh well, pride is contagious, right?

17 Dec 1304 hrs

Had our physical fitness test this morning. It was a little chilly; around forty degrees. Soldiers were all bundled up. The only thing extra I had on was a black stocking cap. I needed this, since I had just shaved my head of all hair. Specialist Birmingham was there, but didn't take the test. Sergeant Pippen, Specialist Joyce, and I all took the test. Joyce failed to run the two miles in the required time. Pippen and I had no problems with the test. Yes, it was cold, it was early, and we are in a war zone. This is where you reach down inside and find the intestinal fortitude necessary to complete the task before you. It is something that can't be taught; you either have it or you don't.

I just returned from having lunch at the mess hall. All those people gave me a headache. I am used to the more intimate dining settings of the coalition building, where I spend so much of my time. Speaking of Building 35, Specialist Franks, who is one of my buddies here, will be leaving at the end of the month to go to Germany. He suffered multiple injuries during a car bombing on the airport road earlier this year. His kneecap was struck by what turned out to be the oil filter from the bomber's vehicle. I'll miss shooting the shit with him, but I'll see him back at Fort Hood next year. First Lieutenant Amy O'Neil is close to buying a house next to Fort Hood. She has been showing all of us photos of her home while describing the parties she wants to have in it. My good friend Roberto Furlani, from Italy, will be coming to Texas to visit us in February. I am planning on taking him to the Super Bowl in Florida. I didn't really come here with the idea of making friends, certainly not those from other nations, but it has all worked out for the best. It really helped at Thanksgiving, and I'm sure Christmas will be the same.

1400 hrs

Oh, I know what my problem is: I am vastly smarter than those in authority over me. I just had a meeting with a marine captain who used the word "evidently" wrong in conversation six times. He meant to say *absolutely* clear; instead, he kept saying, "Are we evidently clear?" After that meeting, I saw a friend of mine, Colonel Reynolds, who is also a marine. We were walking out the front of the palace into a glorious, sunny afternoon. He said, "Boy, Kiver, it is cold out today." I replied, "Are you serious? It's fifty-five degrees. Where are you from, sir?" "South Florida," he said between chattering teeth. Colonel Reynolds is a great guy. He helped me with the Toys for Tots public service announcement last week.

I had so much editing and DVD production to do today. The commanding general here in Iraq, Lt. Gen. Thomas Metz, had his people call my people to produce an edited copy on a news conference he did at the palace. After that I had to do some work for my company first sergeant. He had some filming he wanted me to do. The fact is, I am the only soldier who is a broadcaster working in the III Corps area of operations right now. The divisions down the line have some of their own people, but up here at command level, I am the only one. It is a wonder I get anything done. I really need to get back on the road to film some stories with the troops. Being around all these officers from the palace makes me feel like I'm taking crazy pills. It's like being the janitor at the White House; you see all these people and feel like you could make those decisions.

2300 hrs

Had dinner at the coalition building tonight. The Italian warrant officer, who was also the cook this evening, was dishing pasta onto Lieutenant O'Neil's plate when it gave way, spilling the pasta on the table. He scooped it up and made her eat it anyway. She looked at me and said, "You better not put that in your book." Sorry, Amy!

18 Dec 1620 hrs

Had some amusing experiences with more palace rangers today. I was recording a news conference from VHS to DVD. While it was recording, I went up to the roof to do a live satellite broadcast back to Central Texas. When I came back, a major I know was trying to change the channel on the TV. It wouldn't work, though, because since I was recording, it was locked in. He asked me why the news conference was on TV. I said, "Sir, I am recording from one format to another." "Oh," he replied, "that explains everything." Then later, Lieutenant Colonel Baggio came in and asked the same thing. I said, "Sir, it is not on TV; I am recording from VHS." He at least appeared amused and said, "You got me." It absolutely amazes me that some people can walk and chew gum at the same time.

Provided media coverage for the senior leaders' meeting today. This was a day conference for the representatives of all the coalition partners here in Iraq. This was my second such conference during my time here. They are very worthwhile to attend, as I can hear the views and perspectives expressed by the military leaders of our partners in this conflict. I also enjoy simply meeting the soldiers from around the world. In my case, I know some of them from the missions I have been on here in theater. This is the kind of experience and knowledge that I simply can't get by watching the news every evening.

Got a great lead on a new mission today. I happened to meet the South Korean public affairs officer in our conference room at the palace. I told him I wanted to fly up north to the city of Erbil, which is in the mountains, very close to Turkey. They seemed agreeable to me flying up there and doing a story on the Korean participation in the war on terror. So, cross my fingers; hopefully, first week or two in January, my last big trip before leaving Iraq. Most people crawl into their shell when they are close to going home. Not me; I would much rather be working than counting down the days.

19 Dec 1433 hrs

Rumor has it I have another live shoot this evening with the satellite uplink; however, that was said last night, but it never came to be. I got a letter in the mail from my half-sister, who lives in Oklahoma. I cannot stress enough the importance of getting mail here. The letters she sent were very funny to read. My sister is not well educated at all. She misspells tons of words, which we find very amusing here in the office. Regardless what the mail is or where it comes from, I look forward to it just the same.

I have been interviewing soldiers, asking them how their opinion has changed about the mission since they came here. Here are some of the responses I got, which you will never hear on the network news.

SFC Sherrie Yates, 420th Engineers Army Reserves; College Station, Texas

"The one thing that I think is most vivid looking back at my year here was my first night. We have a tactical radio that allows us to listen to the battlefield updates that commanders give to General Casey about what is going on in their areas. The first time I heard that, I was shocked, because it was such a contrast from the perception you get from the news, living in the United States."

Sgt. Timonthy Jones, 420th Engineers Army Reserves; College Station, Texas

"Well, my tour has been long, it's been trying; there have been good times and bad times. We've lost a couple of people, that's been tough. Being able to be out and see the things I have seen has been lots of fun. A lot of it seems worth it, but it has been tough being away from home. When I first got here, I thought it was going to be much easier than it turned out to be. The people of this country have a long way to go. I think they have had it easy, because their freedom was just given to them. Now they are starting to realize that they have to step up to the plate and fight for what was given to them by the Americans and others. If they don't, well, it will turn out to be a nightmare for them."

I thought it would be appropriate, since my tour is winding down, to hear what other soldiers think about their time here. Those were fun; I'll try to do some more.

2116 hrs

No interview tonight; plans must have fallen through. Nice job, Captain Dunkleberger.

20 Dec 1603 hrs

Filmed a Christmas message this morning given by Lt. Gen. Thomas Metz, the commander of Multi National Corps Iraq. He is a pretty good guy, it seems, far from the concerns of the common enlisted soldier, but that is par for the course with most general officers. He rarely uses my name, but sees me all the time. Brigadier General Formica, on the other hand, is from Fort Sill, Oklahoma. I have only seen him a few times. This morning he called me by name and asked how I was doing.

1900 hrs

The savages were at it this afternoon, launching a few rockets in our direction here in camp. I have a live satellite shoot in one hour, this time for sure. Hopefully, well, maybe—I'll let you know. Best laid plans of mice and men. I received my out-processing paperwork today. Still have over a month, and they already want paperwork. I'll get it done fast and then be free. My trip with the Koreans is still on for going up north in January. That will be a once in a lifetime thing to do. I have begun the momentous task of sorting through photos and videos as well. I've collected so much good material, it will literally take days. I know other soldiers are having the same problem. Everyone, it seems, has a damn digital camera in their pockets all the time.

2300 hrs

Just as I was sitting down to the computer, a rocket came in. Just one, but it shook my entire office. I can't wait until the election draws closer!

21 Dec 1500 hrs

I have lots of paperwork to complete for the shipment of my television gear back to the states. Of course, the customs folks also want to ensure I am not shipping home elephant hair, as we discussed before. This afternoon I am going to interview Army National Guard soldiers from Wisconsin about the time they've spent here in Iraq, as their tour is almost up. These are scheduled for 1700 hrs.

2226 hrs

First things first; today there was an attack up north that killed and wounded many coalition soldiers, including Americans. The mess hall was attacked by rockets or mortars. While these deaths are a tragedy, we are all soldiers. You can't worry about what might happen. I am comforted by the fact that we are winning and killing many more of the enemies of democracy and law than are killing us. I saw some combat footage from a helicopter in Fallujah that killed dozens of armed terrorists in the street—not those eating peaceably, like the Americans killed today. I just spoke to my father on the phone to let them know that I was okay. He asked me if I knew anyone who was killed today. I replied that I hadn't seen the list of those killed or wounded, as that is not released until the families have been notified, although a reporter in Mosul, from Richmond, did his best to notify people by taking photos of the wounded soldiers, which is illegal. I hope he gets kicked out of the country.

In other news, my interviews went well. The soldiers I spoke with are from the Wisconsin Army National Guard. They all work in a medical company here in Iraq, treating the wounded and the sick, regardless of which side they might be on. Here, in their own words, are some thoughts about their time here, as they prepare to return home.

Sgt. Paul Hess

"My thoughts haven't really changed being here. We had to come over here and do our jobs no matter what. I wasn't against the war before I came and I am not against the war now."

Spc. David Kaczmarek

"I got to meet a lot of different people over here and just have a lot of fun. Good times and bad, I just take one with the other. I don't dwell on it. I mean, you are over here for a year, you gotta have fun. I volunteered to come over here and I am proud to serve my country."

Sgt. Tiffany Pfad

"I have two sisters that were serving in Iraq when I first got here. They are both in a military police company. They have both since returned home. I have enjoyed my time here in Iraq and have been able to travel around quite a bit. I was able to work more on my medical skills here in Iraq than in America. Being here I was able to see we do a lot more than is portrayed on the news, as far as helping the local population. I feel we are really helping much more than is shown on the news. I would most definitely volunteer to come back here again. I am trying to get transferred to my sisters' unit so we can all come back here together."

Interviewing these soldiers and hearing their sentiments has really helped me put my feelings in perspective and realize that I am not that different than the rest of the soldiers here, regardless of what we do in the army.

22 Dec 2230 hrs

First things first; I went to the medical clinic this morning to see where the soldiers from yesterday's interviews worked. While I was there, I learned that the first female member of the Army National Guard to be killed in action in three hundred sixty-seven years was from Wisconsin, and from the unit I was talking with. She was a twin herself, and her twin and other sister were in the Guard as well. There was a picture on the wall of the clinic with her photo and biographical information. She was killed in September of 2004 while on patrol in Baghdad.

Now, second things second; had an emergency uplink via satellite with the states today. It seemed that every radio show wanted to interview my commander, Lieutenant General Metz, about what happened in Mosul yesterday. The officers were running around like they were on crazy pills. I was as calm as could be. I had just finished a most relaxing lunch hour in Building 35, with my beverage of choice for the afternoon. We got the shit ready and put the general in front of the camera. I had to tell him to quit moving around. He has a habit of shifting to his left, because he gets nervous. Afterward, he slapped me on the back and told me our army is great because anyone can tell a general if he is doing something wrong. Yeah, right! On my way down the stairs with the equipment, I saw Brigadier General Formica again. He made a little chitchat, which was nice. I was right about him from the very beginning; a great guy, especially compared with some other generals I know.

This evening I was able to watch the interviews that I filmed on the *Today Show* via the Internet. That was very cool, knowing that I was the one running the camera—even though I would rather be in front of it myself. All in good time, I suppose! A couple of hours after that, we did another interview with my deputy public affairs officer, Major Bleichwehl. He did a live shoot back to his hometown in Wisconsin. Apparently, his wife was on the other end. After they did the interview, he sat there talking to her via satellite for fifteen minutes. Jeez, just call her on the phone! Do any of the enlisted soldiers get to speak to their wives live? I don't think so, nor would they let us, even if our hometown stations asked for us. How do I know? Because I tried to set up an interview for myself earlier this fall and it got shot down by Captain Dunkelberger. Surprise, surprise, surprise.

23 Dec 1108 hrs

Packing day for all our gear that is going home via ship. Silliness prevails this afternoon. I can't believe it is only two days until Christmas. We are having a stupid party at the palace on Christmas Eve. I will leave it as soon as I can, so I can go party with people I like, who like me. I am listening to Billy Joel's "Good Night Saigon" on the computer server right now. The apparent suicide bomber in Mosul gave me a great idea. I should go to America and hire Hispanic suicide bombers to come over here and blow themselves up in Mosques. It wouldn't be right, but see how they would like it. If women and children were killed on their streets, maybe they would modify their behavior. If not, at least they would be dying in the same manner in which they choose to kill. In an action like this, certain tactics have an advantage over others. Some people would say that doing this is sinking to the level of those we are fighting. I would disagree. I think my strategy would be highly effective in slowing the use of these weapons in the conflict.

1233 hrs

I still hate the Muslims right now. It is a simple matter of right versus wrong. Call me a bigot, a racist, a supremacist, or whatever you'd like. But when a suicide bomber walks into a place where you live or eat and blows up your friends and family, what will you do? Will you call for understanding like my college professor, Dr. Ernest Gohler, or will you realize your very way of life is under attack? What is a moderate Muslim? These enemies of peace are spreading throughout the world. It is not because they don't have jobs, or resources for a high quality of life; it is because their radical leaders are exploiting the circumstance under which their people live in order to achieve political gain. It is exactly what Hitler did in Germany in the 1930s. When will the collective world wake up and see what is happening? Islam and terrorism are the greatest threats to the world in my lifetime. Does this mean that Islam and Christians cannot live together? No, it doesn't; that is still a possibility. We have coexisted for thousands of years; however, the new breed who oppress women while beheading westerners and raping young boys has to go.

24 Dec 0751 hrs

I was up early this morning to call home and talk to my family. I spoke to my brother for about twenty minutes. My wife and in-laws had gone out to my parents' house for dinner. Well, it is Christmas Eve, and here I sit in Iraq. While I want to stay here as long as I can, I would at least like to be home for Christmas. We have a super stupid work party tonight. Right now I hate all of my coworkers equally, except Staff Sergeant Mattox; he is the world's best straight man. While walking from my tent this morning, I asked two soldiers who had come from chow if they had seen any suicide bombers this morning. Is it too early to joke? What else can you do? They won't let me go out and retaliate.

1316 hrs

Well, the palace rangers changed the time of the party, moving it up by half an hour, with mandatory attendance.

1922 hrs

Bailed from the party. Let's be honest; I am one of the original grinches. At least if I were home, I would be around people that I like. Here, my coworkers are tolerable at the most. At the least, they make me want to stab them. I got out of our party as soon as I could. I headed to my tent to change into my evening wear. Then I am headed to the usual hangout, where I can be with people I like without fear of reprisal for anything I might say.

I did meet a new journalist tonight; she works for the new military police brigade in town. I will go over to their building tomorrow and try to arrange to get on a convoy ride through Baghdad. It's been a while since I rolled on one of those. Seriously, it is very dangerous going out through town, but at this point, I would walk into a terrorist meeting wearing a George Bush mask and just start shooting. I got a letter from a seventeen-year-old high school student in Colorado. In his letter he asked if I could kill lots of Arabs for him. Well, Tyler, I will do my best to kill lots of Arabs for you.

2351 hrs

I hope some Arab cleric reads this and puts out a fatwa to kill me in the name of Allah. Come and get it, you fags! When I talk on the phone to the U.S., I can totally hear when the enemy taps into the phone conversation. When they do, I tell them where to find me, so we can fight it out, yet they never show up. My rage grows every day—seething hatred for the Muslim world. Of course, you must take into account the circumstances under which I live.

I had a wonderful meal this evening with my coalition friends. We had Italian pasta, gumbo, and red beans with rice. Two of the American soldiers are from Louisiana, so that was their contribution. The toast was offered by the gregarious Ukrainian colonel who I really love. He talked about the meaning of the holiday with Christ and all, even though he is Russian Orthodox, which is an offshoot from the Catholic Church. So, while he was giving this toast, a Muslim officer in attendance gently reminded him of his presence, which was appropriate; at least that guy is a member of a coalition country. Just tonight, while I was enjoying a beverage or three watching *National Lampoon's Christmas Vacation*, those fucks threw two rockets in my direction. I mean, Jesus H Christ, you are going to shoot rockets just because it is Christmas Eve? Ask yourself, what would you think and feel if you had the same experiences as me? I hate to beat a dead horse. Well, I did beat a real dead horse once, just to say I had done so. Of course, now I am going to upset the PETA folks. Well, I got news for you vegans, dolphin is delicious.

25 Dec 0019 hrs

Merry fucking Christmas!

1137 hrs

Well, enough time off. I'm going to see people today about getting off this base. The terrorists didn't shell us after the initial attack last night. It's hard to judge what that means in the big picture. As for the home front, today is obviously Christmas. My brother always cooks breakfast for the whole family. It tends to be something outrageous every year that he saw in some cooking magazine. Wish I could be there to put some ketchup on it.

1655 hours

Went over to the new MP brigade headquarters this afternoon. The public affairs office (PAO) captain there said she can get me on patrol on the mean streets of Baghdad. I will be going back over to Building 65 in a few minutes to pick them up and take them to 35 to meet my friends. This way, they can get to know my contacts and friends, since their tour is just starting and mine is nearing the end.

Outside of Building 35 last night, I saw a huge fireball in the distance. I thought I may have had too much water to drink, and didn't give it any thought. This morning I read in the news that a butane-filled tanker truck had been blow up in Baghdad last night. Once again, a witness to the senseless destruction. Staff Sergeant Mattox said I will have to move out to the airport in order to get a good night's sleep when I return home.

2227 hrs

Back in the office, I have no electricity; my computer is running on battery backup. Because of all the rain, our trailer has developed its own electric field. If you touch the door or stand right outside on the step, you take quite a shock. Well, it seems it was too much for the system, so the circuit breaker keeps tripping. I'm sure it will get fixed tomorrow, though. The local server for everyone's Internet runs through our office, so someone more important than me will notice and take care of the problem. I had a great time introducing my new friends to my old friends in the coalition. We even had a sit-down coffee with the Italian general. When we were walking to the car, the captain said how amazing it was for her to meet all those whom I had introduced her to. I can't believe I am actually leaving in a month or so. I still haven't started counting the days. I've got places to go and pictures to take. No Internet tonight. I shall go to my tent and watch a movie, I guess. Ciao!

26 Dec 2013 hrs

Still had no power this morning when I came to work, so I split. I went over to the usual place to use their computers. Did get approved to roll with the MPs through Baghdad, probably on the twenty-ninth of this month; knock on wood, but if the writing style changes, it means I was killed and someone had to finish the journal for me. Well, enough morose thoughts. The niece of a good friend of mine is coming here in January. She is in the Air Force and will be here only four months. Regardless, I said I would call her to give her the lowdown on what she needs to bring and help her get mentally prepared for her duty station.

Mail call was awesome today! My friend Amanda sent me a much needed package for New Year's Eve. The captain has entered the country of Iraq. Thanks, Amanda, you are a great American. I went for a forty-five-minute run this evening. It has been raining, so the roads were really muddy; hard to get a grip with my sneakers. I haven't been to the mess hall since the suicide bombing. Not to worry, I am still eating in the kitchen, plus I nibble on snacks and stuff. If I am going to get killed, I'd rather it be on the streets two days from now than sitting in the chow shoving ice cream in my face. On my walk from the trailer to the office, it appeared that two RPGs were fired at the guard tower that I frequent. Right after that, the soldiers started firing their automatic weapons into the darkness. Crazy stuff. The pagans are trying to scale the fences. We have soldiers walking around with their weapons like it is a fashion accessory. I could name names, but I don't want you to think I am always ragging on people. I am ready; come and get me, you savages!

27 Dec 0028

I am up late watching football. I was over at the building drinking with everyone over there—water, of course. Can't wait till New Year's. So this Baghdad convoy looks like a go. Honestly, I am a little nervous—nervous because I created this mission; no one told me to go. I hope all goes well.

2142 hrs

Had a very productive day. This morning I went with two Estonian officers to watch some of their country's soldiers training in urban warfare. The drive over to the other side of the airport with them was most interesting. I really like foreign soldiers who speak English well. When they can communicate effectively, I really learn what they think about the United States and of the military. For instance, they feel that the U.S. military is too much by the book. The example they cited was if the situation has not been discussed in a manual at the War College at Fort Leavenworth, American officers don't know what to do. I would tend to agree with that. That is a lot of my problem; I think outside the box too much. (There was just an explosion outside my office over by the living trailers.)

Anyway, because I see through some of the bullshit the army does, just because that is the way it has always been done, it pisses people off! However, the two Estonians brought up the issue all on their own. Good for you, guys! I like those who have a bullshit detector turned on all the time.

Learned today that I will be going back out to Fallujah to survey the damage and reconstruction after the first of the year. I am trying to get a good mix of people together for a New Year's Eve party. I have to be careful and only invite those who can be trusted into our "fight club." The first rule is snitches get stitches! Speaking of friends, Specialist Franks left this afternoon. I didn't get to say goodbye. He was one of my drinking buddies (water). He is stationed at Fort Hood, so I'll party with him upon my return. He went up to Germany for surgery on his knee. Lieutenant O'Neil is still getting her new home, so we can all pass out and inspect her tile floors up close. Back to my point; Franks is gone. I know he just got the call from the EVAC medics that they were ready for him to go. Good friends are hard to come by, and good people even harder. Godspeed, and fast recovery, buddy!

28 Dec 1922 hrs

Last night my run was under a brilliant full moon. The lake was aglow with moonbeams, and I was running while listening to Guns N' Roses "Knockin' on Heaven's Door." What a great song. Today I ran in the afternoon under a glorious Iraqi sunset. I was listening to "Have You Forgotten" by Darryl Worley. Why are these songs important? I have an eight-hour patrol through Baghdad tomorrow; odds are good that we will see action. The other journalist going out with me, well, she is a rookie. I stopped by her office this evening and gave her my seasoned vet briefing. I think the thing that surprised her most was when I said, just because an Iraqi has a police officer's uniform on does not mean he is your friend. Trust no one, stay where you can see me and I can see you. She seemed excited and said she is willing to kill first and ask questions later, unlike Specialist Birmingham; but you already knew that. Let's face it; eight hours out in the jungle is a long time to be away from home.

This evening I have to help the Kazzie soldier buy a Sony video camera online. He has a Visa card and is willing to spend money.

I had a very relaxing day. I spent the lunch hour sitting in the sun, then I took a nap, and my aforementioned run.

I have lots of missions coming up. December was painfully slow, with all the stupid parties/ceremonies and Christmas hooey! But eight hours on the road in Baghdad—wow! I am very excited.

2154 hrs

Time to go get some shut-eye. I'm sure I won't sleep. At least I will lie down and watch a movie or something. Ciao!

29 Dec 0500 hrs

This morning I went on patrol with the 127th Military Police Company. We are on our way to respond to a call for assistance from the Iraqi police. They have chased some fighters to their house in a neighborhood on the west side of Baghdad. There are three soldiers in the Humvee with me: the lieutenant, who is the convoy commander of these three vehicles, is from Florida; the driver is a sergeant from Kentucky; and our gunner is from Texas. I asked her if she was one of the crazy Texans who loves Texas. She replied, "Yeehah!" The radio keeps jumping to life, with the lieutenant responding. It is still dark and cool out. I am in a fully armored vehicle; however, the heater doesn't work. What a bitch. Glad I brought a jacket. We pulled up to some other soldiers in the dark to relieve them in place. The lieutenant said that a massive explosion had taken place where we were responding. After we parked the vehicle, I grabbed my camera and we headed to the scene of the explosion. As I walked down the street, the air became heavy with the dust of rubble. The first thing I saw was a fire truck and police tape. I walked under the tape and nodded casually to the other soldiers on the scene. The entire block was absolute rubble. It was still too dark to film effectively. I started walking around, realizing I was walking on what used to be a two-story building. There was screaming and the noise of people digging by hand and by shovel. In a few minutes, once portable lights were installed, the scene became clearer. One corner of the block had completely collapsed. I figured out some of the screaming was coming from the collapsed structure. There were bodies of police officers and others being carried away. More soldiers were arriving—engineers with construction tools. Once the light was better, I was able to start filming. The scene was just like every disaster I have seen on the news relating to the attacks in the Middle East: women wailing and beating themselves in mourning; the men digging with whatever they could. After a couple of hours, someone looked at the rubble that had been blown across the alley. The body of a small female child was pulled out of the pile of bricks. I was standing there filming as an American army medic wrapped a sheet around her tiny body. The bottom of the sheet quickly began to stain with blood. The other journalist with me turned away. This was her first real mission outside the wire, so I don't blame her. Looking into her eyes, I could tell she was bewildered. I actually had to snap my fingers in front of her eyes to bring her back to reality. I said, "Hey, are you okay?" She sad she was, and began taking photos of the scene. As the little girl's body came out and was laid on a stretcher, all I could think was how small she was.

After I left the scene, I called my wife on my cell phone. She asked where I was, and I told her I was at the corner of 42nd and Filth Avenue. I told her about what I had seen, mentioning the little girl specifically. She wanted to know how that made me feel. Obviously, a "how are your fatherhood characteristics" question. My honest response was that I didn't feel anything; I was just shooting video. That little girl was simply part of the daily toll of war. This may be a large flashing sign saying it is time for me to go home to America.

1000 hrs

I have been acting as military police now. We sealed off the neighborhood for safety and security. Unrolled concertina wire blocks the intersections. It seems everyone lives in the house on just the other side of the wire. The ones I feel bad for are the children who, with their bags and books, really are just trying to get to school. My weapon hangs at my side. When I what to get someone's attention, I simply put my hands on it. They then move away. I threw four pairs of brand new shoes to some children. One boy caught a pair, but was pushed in the street, where he sank in human filth up to his knees—a new pair of sneakers his reward. I can't imagine. Another important event happened on that corner. A young Iraqi boy came up to me with something in his hand. "Mister, mister," he cried. I reached over the wire and took what he had. It was an electrical motor—a toy of some kind—and an AA battery. Amazing; this boy had just handed me two components for an IED. He probably saved someone's life by handing me those things. He slipped away back into the crowd, surely not wanting to be seen helping the U.S. in this neighborhood of Sunnis and Baath Party loyalists. The truth is he could have been killed for that simple act, or his family killed in front of him, in any number of horrible fashions.

1100 hrs

I'm on the roof of an Iraqi police station with Private First Class Bigenho, the other journalist. A sense of normalcy is starting to return to her face. We are waiting on the lieutenant, who is in a meeting with the police chief. The motor pool here was quite a sight: police cars with bullet holes all over them, but still roadworthy. Amazing, the resilience of these cops.

1300 hrs

Home, sweet home—back at camp. We pretty much took the freeway all the way back to base. What a commute today has been. I really feel like I've earned the extra pay today. Well, Bigenho said she had a good time, and says she looks forward to going out again, maybe.

2126 hrs

Here is an email from Terence Mann, my former supervisor from the 3rd Army. I will explain his references at the end.

Hey Kiver,
Out of extreme boredom, I read Birmingidiot's blog the
other day. She's complaining to the world that someone
(You) put a damper on her blogging by asking some
strategic questions... Good for you...

I heard they fragged you for something in
Fallujah ... what a bunch of shit! You were the only
one who even attempted to do real public affairs over
there ... but fuck it—3 Corps is a collection of
substandard cocksuckers and losers ... just grin and
bear it and move on... Parris and Morrison fucked me
out of my NCOER and award.
Keep my email and if you need a reference on down the
line, I'll hook you up... I contacted the Force people
about my award and NCOER and they're hooking it
up... I'll send a copy to Parris and Morrison when I
get it back...
Stay safe...

Well, you know who all the people mentioned are in relation to me. Sergeant Major Parris and Sergeant First Class Morrison are my NCOs. NCOERs are forms that are filled out to rate NCOs on their duty performance. It seems that Staff Sergeant Mann has the same view of my unit as I do.

30 Dec 0740 hrs

All last night I was still thinking about what I was involved in earlier in the day. Bigenho, the other journalist, showed me just how shocked people can be once they go outside the wire. Her presence has helped to show me just how far I have progressed in my soldiering.

1701 hrs

I just got an email from Bigenho about the trip we had yesterday. To preface, I had told her that looking back on the events, I had fun doing my job at a scene like what we had seen. This is her response: *"As far as yesterday's trip, I'm glad you had fun. I, on the other hand, have allowed it to have quite an impact on me and would not have brought it up in conversation, if you don't mind ... at least not for a little while. I'm having a rather difficult time coping with what I saw."* I emailed her back, telling her that she was a normal human being having normal feelings. I told her in a few weeks she will be like me and be abnormal when it comes to dealing with violence. I suggested that she use the camera lens as a shield between her and the violence.

31 Dec 0014 hrs

Boy, oh boy, did I play Geppetto with Sergeant First Class Morrison last night. Will see how the situation develops later today. To put it in war terms, she has two IEDs waiting for her at work today: one from a suspected source and one completely out of the blue. Lieutenant Colonel Baggio is my unwitting participant; Colonel Howard is a willing and able accomplice, while the company first sergeant is set for attack mode on my behalf. As Mr. Burns likes to say, "Release the hounds."

I had some Romania fellowship tonight. We were treated to some plum concoction. The Romanian soldier said it was for a sad occasion; he told me later in private it was the anniversary of the death of his father. I'll drink to that. I love being with different cultures. Learning their traditions and mannerisms is something I will take home with me when I leave.

01 Jan 0545 hrs

Up and at 'em bright and early. Will be heading back to bed for a well deserved nap. I have a satellite uplink this morning back to Texas; last year, as it were, ha ha. I am very tired; I poured beverages for all my friends last night, making sure there was not an empty cup in the house, as it were. One new guy I met is a Ph.D. from the University of Denver. When I handed him his cup, he said, "Oh my, a gentleman *and* a scholar."

1531 hrs

Did the satellite uplink thing this morning with my boss, Lieutenant Colonel Baggio, back to Central Texas. While we were there, I was talking to Joyce about how the Sunni Triangle now has a smaller area called the Triangle of Death. How are they ever going to calm these areas down with names like that? He pointed out another place here at our camp. It is called Assassins Gate; it is an opening out to the highway. We agreed these names should be changed to terms like Gate of Prosperity, or Triangle of Opportunity.

At our office party, everyone was given a certificate for their work here. The word professional was misspelled as prifessional. No, I am not kidding; an entire office full of journalists and there is a misspelling like that. Further, our command could have given us certificates of achievement. If they are drawn up correctly and signed by a colonel or higher, they are worth five promotion points. How about that? Our command screwed all the soldiers on this night, not just me. As soon as I left the party, I ripped my prifessional certificate up and threw it away in the trash.

1600 hrs

Sergeant Pippen had a meltdown this afternoon. She freaked out because Joyce has misplaced a memory card for the camera. She walked through the office grabbing stuff off the desk and just tossing it on the floor like so much salad. I was screaming, "It's a meltdown!" She replied by screaming, "I am not having a meltdown." Luckily, she leaves Iraq on the fifteenth of this month. So she will be able to go home and relax.

2300 hrs

My friends all agreed that last night I was single-handedly responsible for ensuring the silliness and staggering of the entire coalition staff. My bosses don't like me hanging out with the foreigners. Unfortunately, there is nothing in the army regulations that mentions spending time with soldiers of other nations.

My friend Amy and I had a good heart to heart talk tonight. We spoke to one another about the issues that come up about going home and what it will be like. Fortunately, it seemed we had similar concerns, like what we will do when we first get to our homes and walk in the door. I am really concerned about those first few minutes and hours of life back in the world. I have a wife to go home to, but I know she will not understand what I am feeling. How could she? No amount of preparedness will be enough to ensure she knows what I am thinking. I can't speak to her about it now, because it will only cause her to worry. I am coming home, but at what cost?

Tonight, in our semi-regular bullshit session, we spoke about what the terrorists may try leading up to the election. I believe, as do others, that the terrorists will unleash everything they have at us. It will be a last-ditch effort. If the elections are even moderately successful, then a whole new way of life will be starting here in Iraq. The president and the United States have gone "all in" at the poker table. It is time for the terrorists to match our bet or fold their hand.

2 Jan 1200 hrs

Slept in like crazy this morning! Well, less than a month till I leave now. Staff Sergeant Mann emailed me and proposed that two thousand people will be killed here on or around Election Day.

We had a satellite uplink back to the Mall of America in Minnesota this afternoon. I will be going back to Fallujah on the sixth, and then the defense minister of Ukraine comes here on the seventh. I am still going out on some more patrols with the MPs in the Triangle of Death.

I stayed up way too late last night. I was pretty slow getting out of bed this morning. Right now we are forming an office pool to bet on how many deaths will occur on Election Day in Iraq. So far, estimates range from two hundred, submitted by Staff Sergeant Mattox, to five thousand, which was my guess.

2238 hrs

The satellite uplink with the soldiers from Minnesota didn't go very well. We had everything ready on this end; however, the TV station truck in America had problems receiving our signal. These civilians who go home to their families and girlfriends every night couldn't figure out the problem until ninety minutes had elapsed. The radio broadcast went off without a hitch. Two radio guys from Minnesota came to Iraq to do a live remote broadcast. Soldiers were able to talk to their families on the phone while I put them in front of the camera at the same time. Once the transmission started working, the families back home could see and hear their loved ones all the way from Iraq.

When we got back to the palace, I had to haul the equipment to the second floor, where it is stored. The elevator was broken, as it usually is, so the only option was hauling it. Birmingham was with me. She is weak, and will freely admit she is weak. I looked at these boxes that weigh over one hundred pounds each, bent down and hoisted it over my head, and walked up the flight of stairs. These are not your nicely American carpeted stairs; these are Italian marble, measured by Iraqi engineers, with a curving path upward. It wasn't easy, but I realized how strong I have become, wearing my gear all around Iraq. I guess lugging around all that stuff on my travels has really paid off.

3 Jan 1418 hrs

We had three incoming rockets at Camp Victory this morning. Ever since then, our artillery units have been engaged in counter-battery, or return fire. It had a nice rhythm going to it. I had been up late and up early, so I needed a nap over the noon hour. The big guns quickly put me to sleep. After that I grabbed some lunch and dined alfresco outside my favorite building. While there, I saw the Italian general absolutely verbally undress the Ukrainian colonel for blowing off a staff call meeting. It was very interesting to see this sort of interaction between our allies.

Earlier this morning I had my medical out-processing to leave Iraq. *Are you depressed? Do you think you have been exposed to this or that? Have you seen dead bodies? Blah blah blah!* Seriously, the whole thing was a colossal waste of time. These are the kinds of things they are worried about? This country is going to come apart at some very big seams before the election. We are doing the best we can, and the terrorists know it. I'm sure they would like to attack us in America before the elections, to show us that they can. I hope they don't, but I am sure they will try.

2200 hrs

I went for a run this afternoon in the declining rays of the day. I wanted to do something different, so I ran to the Baghdad International Airport and back. It is around fourteen miles roundtrip. I didn't think I had that in me. I was wearing civilian shorts, shirt, and sneakers. After wearing a uniform and boots for months on end, putting on sneakers makes me feel like I am flying. It was a flat yet bumpy dirt road most of the way, with lots of traffic to avoid. I was so thirsty when I returned, for I hadn't taken any water with me.

4 Jan 0009 hrs

I was changing the channels last night when some porn movies came on. The coalition soldiers were amused when it appeared on the screen. They told me to change the channel when the general came in. Sure enough, in walked the general. I quickly switched from DVD to TV. This caused the screen to go all white. The general asked me what I was doing. I said, "Oh, I can never figure out these fucking remotes," and started banging on it. Kiver, man of action! Now some may say that watching pornography is crass, but how often would I ever have the chance to watch it with soldiers from several different countries? Here I am, trying to be a diplomat, and someone would judge me for that? Besides, it came on randomly. Why should I be held responsible? It is just the TV.

1108 hrs

Specialist Montgomery just walked out of the office in a little huff. He is the newest soldier to our team. We make fun of him for being the rookie. Pippin and I told him we were going to write nasty things about him in the porta-shitters, so now he is all worried that we are really going to do it.

1521 hrs

Oh my, domestic drama today. One of my Italian friends sent a Dear Giovanni letter to his American love interest here in Baghdad. I can't say I didn't see it coming a long time ago. This kind of things happens a lot during war and deployments; it is just expected. One of the Italian officers tried to explain to me what the Italians are like. I am headed over to the 42nd MP's building to see about my patrols for this week.

1600 hrs

Well, Captain Kierpeck seemed a little annoyed with me this afternoon. She had been planning for me to roll with them on the eighth for a patrol; however, I have a tentative interview that the command put together with Lieutenant General Metz. So I told her I wouldn't be able to go in the morning. She was like, "Well, I can't make any promises that you will get a seat." I said,

"Listen, this is the corps commander; I can't blow him off." She replied, "I don't care who he is, do you know how much trouble it is getting you a seat?" It pisses me off when people act like they are doing me a favor. I am going out on the streets voluntarily to give some press coverage to their troops who are out there every day. I am the one being proactive and doing them a favor. Plus, I want to give the terrorists a few more chances to hit me before I go home. Crazy, yes, but hey, I am a news guy; if nothing happens on a trip, it seems boring to me.

2331 hrs

Had briefings from the chaplain this morning about going home and reuniting with loved ones. There will be a lot of issues to deal with. The biggest that he pointed out is that we are going from seven-day work weeks down to no work, at least for a little while. Other issues are things like intimacy, finances, getting to know each other again. I mean, it's like just crazy. A roller coaster ride for six months and then boom, it's over—get off, have a nice time at home. When I first got here, all I could think of was going home; now all I can think of is staying. Today I was telling my coworkers that if I weren't married, I would sneak back to Baghdad from Kuwait. Just get on a plane coming here. All you need is an ID card. I would come back and travel the countryside every day with my camera. What fun that would be; move right back into my tent and scrounge for things I need, or buy them at the PX. Then, with no chain of command, I could sneak off post with interpreters and spend the night in the city. Oh, what a rush that would be. I am totally serious; this place has grown on me.

5 Jan 1700 hrs

Okay, I just blew up at everyone in the office about repeating tasks or asking the same question seventeen times to get the same answer. Montgomery, the fucking cherry rookie in our office, asked me about a trip that I told him had been canceled. He wanted to confirm that the trip was still canceled. He actually used the phrase "I want to confirm what you told me before." What a waste of breath that was, and a waste of my time as well.

The Ukrainian defense minister will be here tomorrow. One of their officers is telling me at 2000 hrs exactly is when everything is going to happen. Secret squirrel stuff… very interesting!

2300 hrs

Well, two hours went by with my contact not showing up. Finally, a major from that country comes in. I jumped all over him, saying, "Where is this captain?" He ran right out to fetch him. One thing I have learned about coalition partners is it doesn't matter what their rank, they all bow down to Americans because we are the big dog on the block. It really is an amazing phenomenon, which I have proved over and over. Well, the captain finally made it in. He apologized and said he had been in the shower, which was backed up by the fact that he was dripping wet. He told me what time everything was happening so I could be there to film. While I was waiting, I mixed myself two cokes and non-waters, so the time wasn't completely wasted. In other news, I am getting kinda tired of people at home asking me questions about how things are developing here, like I am fucking Colin Powell or something. I mean, I can tell you what I think, but that does not mean it is the gospel. Right now everyone at home is asking about the elections coming up. Hey, I don't speak for the American government, no matter how much I would like to.

6 Jan 1245 hrs

The first thing I want to say about the visit this morning is WOW! Not only was the Ukrainian minister of defense here, but also the ambassador to Iraq and a member of Parliament. I followed the group around for the entire morning. First was a meeting with Lieutenant General Metz, the Multi-National Corps commander, and my boss from Fort Hood. While there, Lieutenant General Metz remarked how much he liked some Polish vodka that he once drank. General Lezmuk laughed it off, but quickly pointed out that Ukrainian vodka is superior; then his aide reached into a briefcase—I thought he was going to pull out a bottle so we could all have a toast. Unfortunately, it was only a statue of a Cossack warrior on a horse. The second meeting was with Major General Weber, USMC chief of staff for Multi-National Force Iraq. He actually offered cocktails out of his cabinet. I took photos just to prove that he had Jack Daniels and other kinds of liquor right there. Remember that prohibition on alcohol applies to all American personnel, regardless of rank. I guess membership has its privileges. A Ukrainian lawmaker spoke frankly about troop reductions from his country. He insisted they would not be like Spain and would only withdraw if the situation allows for it. I really liked this guy, because he was dressed as a soldier and not a politician. I don't like people who come over here in suits. First, you present a great target. Second, I would love to be able to wear a suit myself, but I can't, so show some consideration.

Being able to sit in the meetings was very informative. It allowed me to see firsthand the kind of discussions that happen at the highest level. The defense minister talked about how the events that took place on 9-11 were an attack on the entire peace loving world and not just America. They also discussed the new political climate that exists in Ukraine because of their recent presidential election. These men also gave each other gifts, like all generals do. I gave a gift to the minister as well. I presented him with an American flag and III Corps patches, which I wear on my uniform. I told him I am just an ordinary soldier, but I wanted to give him those things as a friend of the coalition partners and as a thank you for coming to our little party here in Iraq. He said he knew that I was a good and helpful friend of the coalition countries. He also added that it was his understanding that I never missed a party in Iraq. Apparently, someone must have told him about me beforehand, which is a good thing, I imagine. The ambassador was a great guy as well. I asked about getting some good Ukrainian vodka once I get home to America, and he said he could be very helpful in that area. Since having these experiences this morning, I suppose I will be more tolerant of people back home asking me about high level decisions in Iraq, since I did gather some knowledge this morning.

I am so hungry right now. All through the morning I was thinking about the leftovers I had in the fridge here in my office. When I got here, Sergeant Pippin had thrown them out. Savage! Now I have to go to the chow hall for more. Going to the chow hall now is a pain, because they check your ID to make sure you are who you say you are, and they search all the non-soldiers to make sure they are not carrying explosives. Those people shouldn't eat in our chow halls; then we wouldn't have to worry about it.

1600 hrs

My wife's flight was delayed yesterday, so she would have missed the connection in Denver. So she stayed another night to catch the early flight today; however, her ride won't be able to pick her up until 1700 hrs local time in Texas. This means she would have to hang out there for three hours. I would have a blast at the airport, but my wife is not that way. She wants me to call people from the office at Fort Hood to see if they can pick her up. Yes, I will try to arrange that all the way from the Middle East.

2312 hrs

First things first; I will be going out on the streets of Baghdad for another patrol on Sunday. I will be rolling the dice one more time, looking for a seven or an eleven. A Bradley fighting vehicle was blown up in a roadside bombing this evening; seven soldiers were killed in the initial report. It has not hit the news wires yet. According to the email I received from Bigenho, we are leaving at 0800 hrs on Sunday with the 720 MP Company for our patrol. I don't pay attention to how many days I have left here in Iraq. I go home when I go home. I may collapse when I get there, but until that time, there is work to be done.

7 Jan 1042 hrs

Last night I was hanging out with the usual crew; we opened a bottle of Italian non-water, per everyone's desire. While we were doing that, we found out about those soldiers who were killed. It was a little downer for a moment. This morning I am producing a news story for the work I did yesterday to send back to Ukraine. This is in addition to the story I did last weak in Estonia. Apparently, I am becoming very big in Eastern Europe, like David Hasselhoff. My wife got home all right; some classmate of hers from school picked her up, no problem. So that was one less headache to have to deal with here.

1908 hrs

On the aerial attack front, we have not had any incoming for about forty-eight hours. I spoke with my father last night. He said, "Twenty-five days and you will be out of Iraq." I told him I wasn't counting and to quit reminding me. On my way to the office this evening, when I reached into my pocket for the key, I thought momentarily about what it will be like to not need it anymore. I think I will keep it and put it on my key ring back home as a keepsake. There is a new American sergeant major working in my favorite hangout. I sure hope he doesn't put a crimp in our style over there. I sent that video story to Ukraine this afternoon. I even made a joke with the Estonian who works for us. I told him I was popular in Eastern Europe just like David Hasselhoff. He got a good laugh out of that. Just spoke to my wife; she is doing her usual morning routine at the bowling alley. Looking forward to getting out on the town again on Sunday. I heard this little phrase secondhand. It seems a one star general told his staff he didn't want to go out on the streets anymore because he was too close to going home and did not want anything to happen. What a pussy loser! How can one prove that the mathematical probability of getting killed is any higher when you are leaving than it was when you first got here? These people are giving in to their fears. I would rather die in a fiery explosion on the road than get killed walking to the chow hall. Everywhere I look I see dumb people. Well, it is time for me to go have fresh homemade pasta with my friends. Ciao!

2349 hrs

Tonight my wife and I were on the radio together back home. I called in from Iraq while she called in from Texas and we were both on the air together in Spokane, Washington. Isn't that wild? She talked about what it is like to be at home while your husband is away at war. She was very nervous, but didn't sound that way at all. She sounded very sincere and honest, which is good, because that is what she is. I hope people heard what she had to say and take her message to heart. I am headed to bed; I have a satellite uplink in the morning. Then it is the NFL playoffs on TV.

8 Jan 0543 hrs

Up early for the TV shoot this morning. The weather has been very mild for what I would consider winter: forty degrees here, with no wind—I love it.

0757 hrs

Tomorrow Bigenho will be going back out on patrol with me. I hope her professional conduct improves. She seems to have a good attitude and is eager to prove herself. I hope I can instill some confidence in her before I leave the country. I didn't have anyone to tutor me, but I would like to be able to pass something on to the next person. I have to think about going and getting something to eat. I have to attend the daily silliness, otherwise known as the 0900 meeting. I need to go back to sleep!

0920 hrs

Staff Sergeant Mattox dropped his hat in the toilet and is not going to wash it. He said it was just piss, and he doesn't want to lose the sentimental dirt that has built up on it. This has to be one of the grossest things I have seen here.

1835 hrs

One of the other new journalists here in the office is such a cherry little bitch. The company commander wanted him to go on a convoy. The convoy trip is long and dangerous, all the way up to Anaconda, which by helicopter is twenty-five minutes. Well, he told me that there was no story he wanted to cover and that he felt the trip was too dangerous. I said I would go in his place. He told me to go tell the commander. I ran into Captain Snyder outside and related the conversation to him. He kinda chuckled and said

I could go. Later, when I saw this soldier, I told him that I was going in his place and that the commander laughed when I told him why. Well, tough guy changed his mind and said he wanted to go now. So I went back and told the commander. This time, the captain said he didn't want someone on this trip who just had something to prove. I agreed with his assessment that those kinds of soldiers are dangerous. This trip is supposed to be on Tuesday. It is about fifty miles each way through the Triangle of Death.

2316 hrs

I just called some jerk in my hometown who wrote a letter to the newspaper. He wrote it using the personal pronoun we, as if he is here. Strangely, I haven't seen him anywhere in Iraq. People who want to talk like they are here should just come on over. I am sure we could find a spare weapon and uniform over here. Here is some of what he had to say. *"We react slowly to enemy activity and are slow to do so. We destroy towns and discover the enemy vanishes."* Listen, you want to put your misguided opinions out for the public to read? Well, I will take issue with what you have to say. The courts have affirmed this right time and time again. Sue me, and I got something for that, ass!

9 Jan 0017 hrs

Okay, I just got off the phone with Jon. I stand by my previous statements; however, he is a nice guy, as it turns out. He was in Vietnam, so I thanked him for his service, which I think meant a lot to him. He said no one had ever thanked him before. He wanted to know when I would be coming home. I told him I leave February 1, if there is still an airport left. While I was on my run this afternoon, three rockets landed on the airport grounds as I was running by. They came in about half a mile from where I was at the time. It's like I can't even have a jog in peace without these fags messing it up for me.

2150 hrs

Today was a very busy day. I didn't have any time to write throughout the day, like I usually do. I will try to start at the beginning and end at the end.

I woke up at 0645 hrs, stood up and dressed only with a flashlight for illumination, so I wouldn't bother my neighbors in the tent. I was out of the tent in nine minutes. I hurried to the office to check the news and scores from the NFL games. I made it to the office by 0704. I am remembering these times simply because I looked at my watch. I checked the news, my email, and turned on the TV so I could watch the rest of the Jets-Chargers game. I had to be over at Bigenho's building by 0730. I couldn't get away from the game. I left at 0725. I hurried across camp and made it there by 0736. We were being picked up for another patrol through Baghdad, as I mentioned last night. Well, for all my hurrying, our ride did not get there until 0830. We listened to our safety briefing and then jumped in our vehicle. We sped down Route Irish to the Green Zone. On the speedy trip down there, I learn about the soldiers I am riding with. They are in an MP company from Germany. The driver was from Kentucky and the passenger from West Virginia. I don't think I asked the gunner where he was from. On the way down there, we had three cars in a row come at us the wrong way on the highway. I will admit, when I saw the first car, I was sure it was a car bomb coming at us. By the time the third was passed, I just assumed the drivers were drunk. The zone actually has the quickest traffic routes for Baghdad within its walls. Oh, I almost forgot, Bigenho was in the other backseat as well. She, as I remember, is from Pittsburgh. I asked her why she joined the army. Her reason was to get out of her hometown. She was still expressing a lot of freedom this morning about going out. To her credit, she said she would go where she was told, but wouldn't volunteer for missions like this one. In fact, on the way out of her office, a coworker told her to be careful. She said, "I am with Kiver, he is the best!" That was nice to hear. Back to the car ride. So, in and out of the zone and back into city traffic. I don't believe I can accurately describe what it feels like to be riding around Baghdad these days with all of the attacks going on. Every car is suspect; every trash pile contains a roadside bomb. If you want to see or learn aggressive and defensive driving at the same time, come and ride along with any convoy here. We do everything we can to keep from having to stop in traffic: jumping curbs and medians, going the wrong way down the street. No, we hadn't been drinking; for us it is just survival. We pulled into the first police station, but did not stay long. We were off again. The next police station had another platoon of soldiers from the same company there waiting for us. I had brought a bunch of shoes out to the children this time. I got the translator to help me, but as is the case in many foreign countries, most of the children speak English already. I had lots of fun handing out the shoes; Bigenho took my picture. While we were there, an American solider had the symptoms of tetanus take hold; that is to say, lockjaw. His jaw was distended and would not close. They had to take him for medical treatment. That was our ride for the day. We were transferred to the other convoy that had arrived before us. I tell you, if it's not one thing, it's another in this country. After that, we visited two more police stations. We were constantly weaving in and out of traffic; it actually made me laugh, thinking of all the laws we would be breaking back home in the United States if we were to drive like that. At the last station, I interviewed a general of the police force. I asked a lot of very hard questions of him. I do this not to try to hurt him, but to get answers we need, so that I can get others to help him with his problems. Most of the discussion is classified, relating to security concerns and operations. One question that I did ask every Iraqi I could was if they would be voting. All of them said they would, yet they didn't know for which party, because there is no advertising or information coming from the candidates themselves. The people want to participate; they simply don't know how to do it. I really wish I could share with you the concerns the police had about the future of their country. One phrase I kept repeating to the interpreter was, *eventually, the child has to ride the bicycle by themselves.* America can't do everything for you; some day you will have to do it by yourself, and that day is soon, I hope. The general did refer to the terrorists as savages in both English and Arabic without any prompting from me. I laughed out loud with him on that one. I asked about what they do with police officers who turn out to be the enemy. He said, "I would finish them." I asked if that meant killing or executing them. "I swear to Allah that if my own son were a terrorist, I would finish him as well." His son was in the room; that couldn't have been a good feeling at all. I assumed that finishing meant killing, as I don't think it could mean anything else. After my interviews, I went up on the roof. After all, without a target, a sniper is just a crazy with a gun, right? Speaking of snipers, when I was interviewing the general, he pointed out a bullet hole in the wall from the resident sniper. The bullet had passed through his window, over the desk, and into the back wall. I asked where the sniper's position was. He had another officer take me to the back window and point out the building a few blocks away. I leaned out the window and looked for a few seconds; I even waved. Damn sniper must have been on a lunch break. These pagans piss me off. How is it I do these things, drive the same roads as other soldiers, and nothing ever happens to me?

Here is another fact that I learned in my interview from the police. Two months before the invasion, Saddam invited terrorists' leaders and their crew into Iraq and set them up with facilities and money with which to operate. So those who say Saddam doesn't like terrorists, think again. Most of the police leadership are guys who have been doing the job for many years under Saddam. I think they would be in a position to know these things. Today, these cops just want a paycheck, so loyalties switch very easily to the Americans. On the way home it was more crazy driving. Traffic circles are the real bitch. Sometimes you have to go the wrong way, then flip a bitch over the median and come back to get to where you originally wanted to go to.

Today, eight Ukrainian soldiers and one Kazzie soldier were killed when an ammunition pile they were setting to blow beat them to the punch. I learned how to mourn like an Eastern European. First, raise your glass, touch only the hand together with one another, not the glasses themselves, then pour a little on the ground for the dead, and then drink it down in one gulp.

10 Jan 1222 hrs

The interview with Lieutenant General Metz went okay. The show on the U.S. end was with Geraldo on Fox. When we were setting up the equipment in the general's office, a really funny thing happened. We had to lower a cord from the balcony on the third floor, then under the ledge and back up through a second floor window. Captain Dunkelberger lowered a rope down from the window and then closed the window on it so it wouldn't fall all the way. The rope was to tie the cord to, so they could pull it up. Well, I was waiting downstairs to tie the two together. Birmingham opened the window and the cord fell all the way to the ground, landing at my feet. So she had to come all the way down, pick up the rope, and take it back up to the second floor again. Right now I am digitizing my video from yesterday to my hard drive on the computer. This actually takes real time to do, so two hours of tape is two hours of tape. My interviews from yesterday are very interesting to me. I was asking people if they intend to vote in the elections. All of them said yes, but without any real knowledge of the process, as I stressed last night. This lack of information or interest baffles me. I asked Staff Sergeant Mattox about it. He is like a wise old sage at times. He said, "Americans are the only people running on the wheels like hamsters. Everywhere else in the world, people's only interest is chilling out and getting their next meal." When you think about this, it really makes lots of sense.

1531 hrs

For lunch I went for a walk around the lake to relax. The lake is crowded with lots of water fowl doing their own thing. Then the solitude was shattered by two Apache attack choppers flying low overhead. After they passed, a jumbo jet took off from the airport. After the noise died down, I stood and looked at the birds for a while longer. Yesterday I was on the streets in Baghdad; tomorrow will be the same thing. Right now I am looking at the ducks.

2042 hrs

I just woke up from a much needed power nap. I went and gave my official condolences to the Ukrainian colonel tonight. Yesterday he was at the hospital, during the evening. Earlier tonight I walked to where he was sitting in his chair and shook his hand. He stood up to meet me. I embraced him as a son would his father, without any words passing between us. He spoke to his subordinates, offering me vodka to help drown the sorrows, which, as you know, I had to decline. Now this was not ordinary vodka. This was a product of his country, complete with his country's flag on the bottle: a blue band over a yellow band, which means blues skies over golden fields. After mourning with them, I went to dinner with Amy and Federico in the chow hall. Soon after, I realized I had to sleep off some of my mourning from earlier, which brings me to where I am now.

11 Jan 0003 hrs

Just about ready for bed; I'll say it now to make it so by morning time. We haven't been shelled in the last thirty-six hours or so. Here that, you fags out there in Baghdad? I am talking to you! I'll be sleeping peacefully in tent thirty-nine; feel free to come and get some.

0613 hrs

The savages must have read my mind. Rockets started coming in at 0046 hrs and continued every seven minutes for about an hour. This morning the first rocket came in at 0530, then the call to prayer began at the local mosque. How convenient.

Well, I leave for my road trip through the Triangle of Death in forty-five minutes or so. I will write when I get back. I still have lots to say about my trip two days ago. "Here I go again on my own."

2028 hrs

Back from my road trip up north. We had our usual safety briefing before leaving. My gunner wanted to have my M-16 on the roof, so he traded me his fully automatic machine gun. It is the same caliber as my 16, but it is belt fed, and has a bipod on the front. The other journalist with me was so jealous. He took several pictures of me with it; then I told him to beat it. He even asked me if I knew how to use the weapon. I responded that I did in fact know how to use all of the crew served weapons. I made sure that I had these skills in case my gunner was ever shot and I had to jump up from the backseat and start returning fire. So I had this machine gun in my lap; as I said before, I don't get an erection over weapons, but this was still pretty cool.

The drive up was fairly eventful. Several Hummers in our convoy struck civilian vehicles that were either stupid or were trying to get too close to us. Either way, it was a real demolition derby on the highway this morning. You might not quite understand. If someone gets too close to us, we simply run them off the road. There will be a lot of bodywork needed in this country. We have to behave this way because of the threat of car bombs. It is either hit-and-run, or face the possibility of being blown up. A more drastic measure is to shoot the oncoming vehicle if they are moving at a high rate of speed. My gunner did that on the trip back. We were the last vehicle in the convoy. He started screaming at the driver behind us to stop, but he didn't listen and paid the price with two .50 caliber rounds in his hood. After that, my gunner was fired up, cackling with laughter the rest of the trip. He didn't kill the driver, or the car; he just let the man know that we are not to be trifled with in this environment. Meanwhile, I was looking out the window. I saw a little boy waving at us halfheartedly. I waved back. He saw me and I could see his spirits soar and his arm stiffen as he acknowledged me. Those are the small victories that keep me going. Iraq's fields are also becoming very green with the spring crops already. It reminded me of the winter wheat that grows back home in Washington this time of year. Tonight I am not going to say we haven't been shelled, because of what happened last night. I will simply go take my shower and go to sleep. I am trying to get to bed before 0000 hrs tonight. This staying up late and getting up early really taxes the body. Of course, I have an interview at 0600 hrs tomorrow. Figures.

12 Jan 0902 hrs

No interview this morning; it was canceled before I went to bed. That was a nice treat, considering I still didn't make it to bed until after midnight. Today is a busy time, trying to finish all the projects I have in the hopper from my recent trips. To complicate matters, it appears it will be a nice, sunny day, which brings on cabin fever.

2038 hrs

Today was another great example of how poorly my command operates versus how well the others that I work with do. The 42nd Military Police Brigade out of Fort Lewis, Washington, is the unit I have been going out with lately. Their commander, who is a full colonel, had asked to speak with me earlier in the week. No one knew why he wanted to speak to me, including Bigenho. When I was over there, Captain Kierpeck took me into his office. He was a nice looking white haired guy, probably close to fifty years of age. We sat down and he simply asked me to tell him what I had seen on my trips and could share from a public affairs perspective. I was very impressed with his candor and instantly felt we had a good rapport based on the amount of respect he was showing me and my opinions. I managed to sneak in a few good comments about Bigenho and her potential as a journalist. I wish my own command would show me half as much consideration as this stranger did to me.

As of right now, I am going to forever refer to Bigenho by her first name, which is Laura; it is just much easier to write. I have written much about her already. I will add a few things here. She is about as dysfunctional with computers as I am. We had a helluva time copying her photos from the hard drive to my thumb drive. Her boyfriend is also in Iraq, serving somewhere up around Mosul. She is a tiny little thing. I tell my friends she would fit in a pocket, if you had to carry her. I hope she continues to screw her head on straight when it comes to missions. She told me that the last time we were driving through the city streets, she thought we were going to be killed by the natives milling around our vehicle. Crazy kid!

Was walking over by the coalition building earlier when Specialist Maxim stops me and says, "We have a goat out back." Sure enough, we walked around the corner and there is a savage Iraqi long-haired goat. I walked right up to the buck and started petting him. The stench coming off his hair was very strong, but reminded me of the farm I grew up on. Having some skill in animal medicine, I looked him over for a quick health evaluation. I'm sure the thing has worms, but his feet also needed trimming. I told Maxim I would go get a knife and come back. When I returned, I managed to trim his hooves down quite a bit. See, goats have toenails just like humans. If they are not trimmed or worn down, they fold over on themselves and become uncomfortable for the animal. So I did my good deed for the savage animal. Americans are not allowed to keep pets, so Maxim is saying he is food intended for consumption. We will see how long this lasts. I am sure some palace wiener will see him and raise a big fuss. Regardless, it was nice to pet and help an animal here in Iraq. Just a touch of home for a farm boy like me.

2312 hrs

I swear, tonight I want to be in bed before the bewitching hour. One last story from today; for dinner I went to the mess hall. We have to show military ID now to prevent foreigners from blowing us up. The soldiers on duty were from my unit, and I have a casual relationship with them. I walked by and flashed my driver's license to see if they were paying attention. I got two steps past when one of them said, "Hold on, Kiver." At least they are kinda paying attention.

Good night, not good morning.

13 Jan 0927 hrs

I did make it to bed before the morning last night. It was so nice to get a good night's sleep. Today is more organization of the office: sending out photographs and stories, getting paperwork in order. I also have to go see how the goat is doing. Plus, we have a satellite uplink this afternoon. On top of that, I want to work on my tan again over lunchtime, since it is a nice spring day again.

1329 hrs

While walking across the street to the palace compound, I saw a Humvee pull up and drop off a soldier, then drive away. I told this man that I can't wait to be at an airport back home and ask a stranger for a ride to wherever I need to go. Surely they will tell me to screw off. Here in Iraq, everyone helps each other out with a ride if it is needed. I've picked up several people that I saw walking, if they were going my way. Back home, would you pick someone up on the airport road? I mean, you know where they need to go—you are going to the airport—yet you'd probably drive right by. There is something for you to chew on right now.

2048 hrs

Just about everyone from III Corps and Fort Hood has moved back into the tents. They had to get out of the trailers to make room for the new soldiers coming in. A few people I know have seen me around the tents and made some comment about having to move back in to them. I replied, "I have been in the tents the entire time. A trailer came open and I didn't want to go." To explain, here is a list of reasons why a tent is better than a trailer: People haven't been killed in a tent yet; in trailers, yes, they have. Tents don't get shelled. See reason one.
In the tents, rank does not apply, seniority does.

Tents are close to the showers, food, and work.

Tent mates are temporary; trailer mates are for the whole tour.

Tents are unsecured, no locks. If one wanted to have a distillery, a porn stash of any other illegal activity plausible, deniability is what you want.

Heck, it's just like camping.

There is more room for me and the rats to share rather than fight one another.

No drama of living with people you know from home, spying, or ratting on one another, like in the trailer park.

It is like being in your own *M.A.S.H* episode.

There you have a few of the reasons why I never moved into the mortar magnets known as the trailers.

2340 hrs

I just watched a pretty good movie with Federico and Amy. Federico said I may come visit him in Italy whenever I want and that he has lots of room for us to stay. God, some days I really love this war. I did some grazing in the mess hall for the goat tonight. I got him a big plate of vegetables and took it over to where he is tied up. This goat seems pretty friendly; he has even bleated at me once or twice. Growing up on a farm, it is a nice distraction to have an animal around here. As for the attacks, there was one mortar round that came in this morning and two so far tonight.

14 Jan 0917 hrs

When I talk to my friends and family on the phone now, they all want to tell me how many days until I leave Iraq. This pisses me off, because the army will most likely send me back here within the year. I would rather stay longer on this deployment than come back for another one. Now, any war haters out there, don't get too excited; I will serve where I am told and enjoy doing it. It's leaving home that is the hardest. As I said before, watching my wife walk away was the hardest thing I have ever done. Right now I am having a great morning. I mean really great! I slept well, the sun is shining, and I just cranked out a two-minute story in nothing flat. Since it is such a nice day, I am going to go for a run.

2217 hrs

I had to send my story out on the satellite uplink this afternoon. Then I went for a run and a swim. Winter is over. I dove right in the Aussie pool. The water temperature didn't even shock me. I swam laps for about twenty minutes. Some people did take my picture, because they are wrapped around the calendar instead of the weather. The goat was butchered today. I saw his carcass hanging up. Of course, to a farm boy like me, there is nothing more natural than eating something that once was your pet. I can look the animal in the eye and still enjoy the meal. I called Federico tonight to see when we would be watching a movie. Immediately, he asked, "Where are you?" I said, "I am on the phone." "Come over right away, we have made pasta; it is dinnertime." I hung up the phone before he was finished, and burst out the door! The only time I ever said no to a free drink or meal was when I misunderstood the question.

Yesterday, one of my officers, Major Bleichwehl, made fun of himself. I like people who can do that, especially when it is true. He said, and I quote, "I have D.A.B.S., which stands for Dumb Ass Bleichwehl Syndrome." I really enjoyed hearing him say that!

2320 hrs

Sometimes when I stop what I am doing and really listen to the sounds here, it is amazing that we get any sleep at all. I'm still in the office, but the sounds are all around: helicopters constantly flying overhead, gunfire, random explosions. I mean, it is crazy! Like nothing I have ever experienced before.

15 Jan 0021 hrs

I have to be awake in a mere five hours. Interviews, the old morning routine, as it were, then once again the silliness known as the 0900 meeting—mandatory attendance; no swimming as an excuse. Good night!

0826 hrs

Just returned from breakfast with Staff Sergeant Mattox and our new satellite boss, USMC Lieutenant Shultz. While eating, Colonel Howard came over and joined us. The whole time, he was the leader of the Kiver glee club, going on and on to this new lieutenant about what a great soldier I have been and an asset to the Corps. On our way out, I grabbed about six juices. Colonel Howard said, "If I didn't know any better, I'd say you were getting supplies for a distillery." I replied, "Sir, I am shocked, nay, I am appalled that you would suggest I am involved in any behavior like that in my tent." Yeah, right!

2000 hrs

Had an awesome run and swim this afternoon. I am heading to bed early so I can get up and watch football. The playoffs start at 0030 hrs tomorrow morning, so I have to be up and at 'em.

0130 hrs

I am up and doing things here in the office. I am watching football, of course. Plus Joyce is still here too, bouncing around, acting the fool. We are actually having a pretty good time. He is filling out tons of online dating surveys so he can go home and ya know, get it on. Yesterday, Sergeant First Class Morrison asked me to do a video project for D.A.B.S.; however, through some investigation, I found it had already been done by our public relations firm. It was just some editing of fifteen DVDs, to pull off the best video and put it on one. I have told the palace rangers repeatedly that no one here, not combat camera nor I, had that kind of software, yet they don't want to listen to me at all. I mean, seriously, I looked right at her this morning when she handed me the CDs and said, **"I don't have the software to do this! No one here at Camp Victory can do this!"** Of course, she just ignored me, as usual!

No incoming rounds tonight. I know that is good, but always disappointing. If I were a terrorist, I would be getting desperate. The election is coming, which means my way of life is ending.

16 Jan 1302 hrs

While sitting outside my tent this morning, I began thinking about the terrorists outside the wire, knowing that they are planning mayhem and destruction in the upcoming days. It has been rather quiet lately. I'm sure it is the calm before the storm that is sure to come in the next two weeks. It is an eerie feeling knowing that there are people out there plotting your death, even in an abstract way. When I was out there, one of my old tent mates came by and asked where I was on New Year's Eve. I told him, and he was disappointed that he missed the party where I was. It was funny that he knew I would know where the parties were.

2036 hrs

I am burning a copy of Sergeant Dima's funeral to tape right now. He is the one American soldier who was killed soon after getting his citizenship. The senior Romanian military officer requested a copy from me. It just so happens he is one of my hydration buddies from Building 35. I didn't think I still had it on my hard drive. I was working on Colonel Howard's dozer film when I stumbled across it. I am really glad I found it, because every time this officer saw me, he would ask for it. He is a really good guy. He calls me Senator Kiver whenever he addresses me. I like that; very Romanesque. I think what I have enjoyed most on my tour here has been the interaction with our Allies. This is, after all, the global war on terror, not the American war on terror. I have learned so much from our Allies, not only militarily, but culturally as well. I can now make jokes in other languages, and most importantly, I can understand when they are being made as well.

17 Jan 0055 hrs

I have some interviews I did with some Iraqi citizens about the upcoming vote that I will try to get onto paper. They shared some interesting thoughts with me that I would like to pass on. I was just talking to my aunt in Cleveland via a calling card, when I ran out of time. Usually, you get a one-minute warning tone or something; didn't happen this time. Oh well, it's not the end of the world.

1445 hrs

Lots of DVD making this morning, as I'm trying to get copies of everything out to the people who need it. I have been looking at airfare on the Internet; fares are silly cheap. It is amazing what the price war is doing. Well, with all the military people coming home, they will be sure to do a lot of business. I have to run now and deliver some video products to those who need them.

2048 hrs

Colonel Howard is coming over here to check out the video project on his dozers. The project is about sixteen minutes in length. I like this guy, and he is my friend; I hope he likes what I have done with the footage. He wants to show it at some Marine Corps Engineer convention this year. That is good for me; lots of people will see my work, which I like. I'll wait and see what he thinks of my work so far.

2228 hrs

Great news: Colonel Howard loved my work! Tomorrow I am going to film a short piece with him adding his two cents worth about the project, to add on at the very end. Plus, he is going to call Sergeant First Class Morrison and put in several good words for me about my work, which I could really use, although I am certain she will ignore them all, or will ask why I am talking to a colonel. Such is life, I guess! Overall, I feel really good about the whole thing. It is nice to still be working while other people are just sitting around doing nothing.

18 Jan 0100 hrs

Just got off the phone with my wife. We are trying to make all these travel plans for her college graduation, my vacations, and her family coming to visit. It's like I am taking crazy pills. I need to walk home to my tent. It was so dark last night, with no moon at all. I found my way, because right now, this is still home.

1010 hrs

Tons of rumors going around right now: some about the election, others about what we are doing in Iran right now as far as covert operations and such. It is fun to speculate about yet serious issues all at the same time. I don't disagree with the president's policies at all. I do disagree with policies farther down the line, as you know.

1746 hrs

Had a great afternoon. I went out with Colonel Howard and let him say a few words for the video. Then we went up to the palace and he said wonderful things about me to Lieutenant Colonel Baggio and Sergeant Major Parris, separately, for maximum impact. Thankfully, Sergeant First Class Morrison wasn't there to ignore all the good things he had to say. Picked up the portrait of my wife today, as well as some Iraqi soccer apparel for my brother. We have a new marine in our office; his name is Corporal Ramsey. I was walking around introducing him to important people in our world, when we came upon a funny scene. It seems one man somehow fell in the moat. After we realized what had happened, Ramsey started laughing out loud at the guy, it was so funny. I mean, in the middle of the day, falling in the water. I have been careful some nights when I was too hydrated to give the moat a wide berth, but in the afternoon... come on. You would have to be a moron.

2236 hrs

I ate some of the goat tonight—yum yum. Amy wouldn't try any, because she had met the goat while it was still alive. Ramsey came over to the building tonight. I think he shall be my social replacement when I leave. He brought liquid refreshment with him as well. Good form, old buddy, good form. Well, I am trying to make it an early night this day. We shall see if I do. Sometimes it is so hard to leave the office, which is free of distractions at this time of day.

19 Jan 0818 hrs

Came in to the office early and did some work. I was talking on the phone, and a mortar round came in close enough to shake the trailer. I was sitting at the desk with my feet up and it didn't even phase me. Seriously, I was talking on the phone when the explosion happened. I said, "That fucker was close," and continued with my conversation.

1423 hrs

Sometimes I really love being in the army. This morning I was walking out of the palace gate when an army major called me over. He asked if I could escort him and two others into the palace for a tour. They didn't have the proper badges, so they needed someone to be with them. I grudgingly agreed, since I do work in public affairs. I walked around with these soldiers and learned they were all from a National Guard unit in Louisiana. Since I have traveled in that state quite a bit, we had lots to talk about. I told them how I would really like to retire down south of New Orleans. As I was talking, I began to realize that all of the great experiences I have had over the last two years were derivatives of my army service. Even my time here in Iraq, although dangerous, has been enjoyable. Basically, I have been paid to tour an entire country in six months. I have lived in America for more than twenty-five years and still haven't seen it all.

1816 hrs

Went for a run this afternoon. When I got to the pool, there were three people there already. Ah, I remember the good ol' days when it was just me. *Where have you gone, Joe DiMaggio?* I walked around camp today with the video camera, recording everything I had seen throughout the day; that way, I can give a walking tour to my friends and family back home upon my return. I had wanted to do this for some time, but it now is starting to hit me that I am going home sooner rather than later.

2148 hrs

Have an interview in the morning. Will try to make this an early night, maybe even before 2300 hrs.

20 Jan 0535 hrs

Made it to bed early, but sleep didn't come. Then at 0044 hrs, someone's alarm went off for about five minutes; he must have been in the bathroom, because I heard him come in and shut it off. I won't miss my roommates when I'm back home, but then I will have my two cats to deal with.

1119 hrs

Had a great interview this morning with my favorite general, General Formica. He is a really great guy who tends to be very engaging with the soldiers around him. He even thanked us all for getting up early to put him on television back to Oklahoma. I like it when the higher-ups take time to notice what we little people do for them.

The call to prayer seemed rather aggressive this morning. No attacks yet. Yesterday we were fired upon twenty-four times throughout the day.

1600 hrs

One of my Italian buddies asked if I could lend some of my "movies" to him for some of his soldiers who are sick right now, to help them pass the time. I asked, "Well, what kind of movies?" He said, "You know what kind they want." Noting the lessons I learned from watching every episode of *M.A.S.H.*, I said no problem, but told him I would require something to soothe my throat in return, and thus a deal was brokered. I should work for the State Department. Further evidence of my diplomacy was yet to come this day. The Ukrainian Colonel Ushakov asked for a photo I had taken with him and his minister of defense. I quickly ran to my office, grabbed my thumb drive, and returned with the pictures he desired. Sitting at his computer, he gave me photos that he had taken of me. He had several pictures of me presenting his minister of defense with an American flag. I was pleasantly surprised; I hadn't known that these photos even existed. Another exchange with a foreign representative here in Iraq. I think I'll call Dr. Rice and ask her for a job.

2020 hrs

I'm watching the president's address to the nation right now. I could have been there in D.C. today with my contacts. Instead, I am here taking part in the freedom of others, being a part of something bigger than me. When the president uttered those lines, I felt like he was talking to me. I am part of something bigger over here. Regardless of the circumstances, we have lifted millions of people out of bondage and terror.

21 Jan 0136 hrs

Time to go to bed. Lots of helicopters still flying around tonight, out hunting bad guys, I'm sure.

1106 hrs

Was supposed to go pick up a reporter on the street outside the gate this morning. It was canceled/postponed, for reasons unknown to me. Oh well, no love lost for me. One of the new soldiers from Fort Bragg hung a Washington State flag up on the wall of our office yesterday. He is from the Seattle area, but it was still cool of him to hang the flag up. I approve of his action.

2010 hrs

The final product for Colonel Howard's dozer film is cutting to tape right now. Finally! This thing has taken forever. On the war front, lots of mortars came in this afternoon, landing over on the airport grounds. I was running out in that area and was able to watch them as they sailed in for impact. It was quite a sight watching them arch across the sky and explode harmlessly in the dirt. Seven rounds came in during this particular barrage. All people can talk about now is the election and going home. There are tons of rumors going around camp that we may not be leaving because they will be closing the airport for a few days. Having the army keep me here so I miss the Super Bowl was not what I meant when I said I wanted to extend my tour. I want to stay and keep working, not sit here on my ass waiting to go home.

2311 hrs

Pirates of the Caribbean with my buddies at the usual hangout tonight. Watching movies with foreigners is really funny, because they don't understand many of the references being made. I always have a really good time because of these cultural differences. I had dropped off the tape for Colonel Howard and left the number of where I was watching the movie, so he could call me. It was Federico's number. So his phone rings and he goes for it. I said it may be for me, and of course it was. He held out the phone for me. I apologized and said, "The war simply can't go on without my constant consultation." HA! HA!

22 Jan 0048 hrs

I decided I am going to get some bumper stickers made for commercial distribution in the states. They will say in both English and Arabic, "Stay back 150 feet or you will be shot." I talked to a friend in my hometown who owns the local feed store and he said he would sell them at his business. I'll be sure to send one to the ACLU with a press release so they get all pissed off and raise a fuss. Here is what it will look like. Remember, Arabic reads from right to left. **Stay back 150 feet or you will be shot ???? ????? 150 ????? ?? ??? ?????? ??? ?????**

1030 hrs

The television station really pissed us off this morning. We had a colonel in front of the camera and were told we were going on at the beginning of the show. Instead, they put us on at the end, so we all had to wait twenty-five minutes. After that, it was the 0900 silliness, which because Lieutenant Colonel Baggio was forty minutes late, pissed everyone off. He had specifically said everyone had to be there today, yet he shows up late. If that isn't symptomatic of the problems in our office, I don't know what would be. In fact, as I was walking back to my tent this morning, I was thinking of all the mistakes and pratfalls that have occurred because of the palace rangers. Oh, they will say they have told the story of Iraq through the embedded reporters they have facilitated; unfortunately, they allowed these reporters to tell the story the way they wanted. If the journalists in our office, including me and four others, had been allowed to do our jobs, it would have been much different. No, I'm not bitter. I feel bad for the soldiers who gave there lives while the folks back home were misinformed about what was really going on here in Iraq.

1845 hrs

The weather has been so shitty here all day long—cold rain mixed with high winds. The water makes terrific mud here in the desert; it clings to everything, including itself, making big globs on your boots. I think I will return to my tent and watch some DVDs in bed. I have guard duty at the chow hall for all meals tomorrow. I hope the weather improves. It will be miserable if it rains all day.

23 Jan 2051 hrs

I've been doing my guard duty at the chow hall today. I only have one meal left, which is chow from 1100 to 0100 hrs. It has been fairly boring, except for turning people away who violate the rules. Examples are people coming in without ID cards or not having their weapon on safe. The funniest thing was telling the females it was ladies' night in the chow hall, all drinks half off! Hurry up and get drunk; I don't like to work hard.

24 Jan 2120 hrs

Have been very busy packing up the office and all the equipment. I did want to share some things that happened today. This morning I was cleaning my tent while another new soldier was in there with me. We were talking, when a rocket came in and landed about a kilometer away, based on the sound. This guy jumped in the air and screamed, "Oh shit!" I said, "Relax, Sergeant Kiver is here; I won't let anything happen to you." Rookies—never a dull moment when they are around. After that I had to pick up some CBS journalists out on the highway and give them a ride to the airport to catch a flight up to Mosul. While they were both Americans, the female lives in Jerusalem and the man lives in Prague. Needless to say, we had a very interesting conversation about the state of world affairs, exchanging ideas and solutions. Then this evening I had a satellite shoot back to the states. Birmingham asked me not to use her name in my journal. I told her she could sue me in court and try to show a judge and jury how I have caused her harm by writing the truth. Then she tried to tell me I can't write the things I have written because I am still in the army. I replied that not only have I read the regulations, but that Lieutenant Colonel Baggio is the approving authority who, by the way, has no problem with my journal or what I may have written about him or others. I think Birmingham is simply worried about all the things she has done and what others might think of her because of these facts!

Lastly, the mailman was good to me today. It should be a very happy evening!

25 Jan 2000 hrs

I had a very fun evening last night with my usual friends; however, it was so much fun that I quickly became very depressed that I am leaving to go back home. I have not been eating or sleeping well at all lately. When I brought up my health concerns to my chain of command, guess what, they didn't believe me. Instead of getting professional support, I was criticized and disbelieved.

26 Jan 1849 hrs

I am still feeling down today. I had an interview with Geraldo this morning that went back live to Fox News. It wasn't any big deal, but the bosses were all over Geraldo's balls and kissing his ass. Just another day at work for me. When I was doing the sound check with the folks in Atlanta, I said, "Hello, Atlanta, I will be at the Super Bowl in Jacksonville. Where are the Falcons?" Geraldo asked, "Is he really going to the Super Bowl?" Lieutenant Colonel, Baggio said, "Oh, Kiver is one of the best broadcasters in the army." Blah blah blah. Geraldo wasn't even listening at that point. It was very amusing to see the boss getting ignored.

27 Jan 2112 hrs

My good friend Staff Sergeant Mattox left Iraq today to travel to his home station in Alaska. He was the only one here I worked with that I really called my friend. I will miss him and hope to visit him and his three grizzly bear children some day. This evening I am watching *The Three Stooges* with my friend here at the usual place. Amy is very upset, because a college mate of hers died in a helicopter crash in Kuwait. He was an Apache pilot who was doing his gunnery qualifications before coming to Iraq. I didn't know what to say to her. She had been crying, but as you know, I am not the most sensitive, and even less so right now.

Earlier this afternoon I punked out a fellow soldier at the mess hall. I had heard through the grapevine that he was talking shit about me. I went and confronted him, because my bullshit detector is set to maximum right now. Since I had the initiative, I could see the terror in his eyes, as he refused to back up to my face what he had said behind my back. A grown man not willing to step up and say what he feels—fucking pussy! I am sure I won't be easy to get along with back on the streets for quite some time.

28 Jan 1302 hrs

Had to get the folks in charge of the tents to sign off on my clearing papers today. To do this, I packed up all my shit and moved it into another tent; then they signed and checked to make sure I was gone. Later I will go back and move my stuff into my original tent, where I am most comfortable. The whole thing is just silly. I leave in a few days; why should I have to move to another tent to make KBR folks happy? For lunch, I cooked Cajun food in the kitchen. Corporal Ramsey joined me for lunch as well. We went to the mess hall to do some grocery shopping and then returned and set to work on the ragin' Cajun feast. Tonight I have a satellite shoot at 2100 hrs and then another one in the morning at 0600 hrs. No rest for the weary, I guess!

2341 hrs

Just got done watching some more *Stooges* videos with Amy and Federico. They didn't like the *Stooges*, so we were talking about funny things that had happened today. When we were in the kitchen at lunchtime, Colonel Ushakov came in following his nose and asked what I was cooking. When I told him, this is what he said: "I didn't know you were a cook; I thought you only knew how to drink!" Then Amy and I started talking about how America provides so much food to the rest of the world. She asked, "Why can't other countries figure out how to grow their own food? Something will grow in every region of the world. Why are we the only ones who have figured it out?" So we are having this funny conversation about our day with the *Stooges* still playing, when Amy asked if I had been drinking a lot of water, as I appeared to be overhydrated. My honest answer was,

"No, I just really like the *Stooges*." Well, it is getting to be bedtime, so I think I'll start walking that way.

29 Jan 2046 hrs

I made dinner tonight for all my friends. I prepared a Cajun meal that was really yummy and fed about twenty of my friends. It was my way of giving back for all the meals that I have eaten here in this building. On the war front, attacks are really spiking this week, as the election is tomorrow. There were lots of attacks just today, as the curfew doesn't seem to be working. The bad guys just go about their business as usual. There have been explosions all evening, with U.S. jets patrolling the skies above.

30 Jan 2034 hrs

Great day for the Iraqi people and those who love freedom around the world. I am so happy that the election went well, with a minimum number of deaths. The big losers today are the terrorists and Saddam loyalists. God bless those soldiers who gave their lives in this endeavor to bring freedom to the Iraqi people. May God bless President Bush as well for having the courage to send American and Coalition troops here to complete this very important task.

I met Peter Jennings this afternoon. While I disagree with his politics and opinions, it was still an honor to speak with him. He asked me how long I had been in Iraq and when I was leaving. I answered him and said I wouldn't mind staying longer. He seemed surprised; as I am sure he wanted me to say I was scared or lacking in body armor or something.

31 Jan 2100 hrs

Had lots of last minute packing to do today as well as saying my last minute goodbyes, which were very hard to deliver. I am not going home; I am leaving home once again. This means I have left home twice in the last seven months.

Birmingham kept me up in the palace doing paperwork this evening when she knew I had plans for my last evening in Baghdad. Finally, I got out of there around 2200 hrs and was able to go over to the usual hangout.

01 Feb 0100 hrs

Corporal Ramsey had been waiting for me for over an hour. We went inside to grab a drink. Federico had presented me with a bottle as a gift the night before as a going away present. As it was already late, everyone was on their way to bed except us. We started in the kitchen, but after a couple of glasses, I realized we could go into the living room and watch movies without disturbing anyone else. We stayed and destroyed the entire bottle while watching *Beavis and Butt-Head* videos. I have to head to bed now, as the morning comes early. This is the day I will leave Iraq—at least for now.

1424 hrs

Today has been very crazy. We had to get all of the bags loaded and ready to go. We left for the airport at about 1300 hrs. Now I am at the airport waiting for our air transport to Kuwait. I am not really excited about going home yet. I finally realize just how much I have embraced the craziness this country thrusts upon those who live here. I did this in order to cope with my situation. Instead of worrying and fighting my reality, I simply became a part of it. This is probably hard for you to understand, but it is the truth.

2019 hrs

We are in a convoy of buses sitting on the side of the highway in Kuwait. We were briefed about a possible suicide vehicle attack here in this country. I have ammo in my weapon, as does one other soldier on the bus. Right now I feel more vulnerable in this country than I did in Iraq. At least there we had a fighting chance; here we are sitting on the side of the road in a big bus that everyone knows is full of unarmed soldiers. Just because the curtains are drawn doesn't mean that the bad guys don't know we are here.

2 Feb 0015 hrs

Finally, I am in my bunk and settled in for the night. There are hundreds of soldiers sleeping in this big hangar; some going to war while others are going home. Needless to say, it is an absolute zoo in here. People are coming and going so much they don't even turn off the lights. At least I am no longer in Iraq, so I guess that is something.

0945 hrs

I was sleeping soundly when a soldier came in and started yelling, "Everybody up, get up, clean your bunk up!" Crazy, I had nothing to do all day, so I just rolled over and went back to sleep. I did get to see one soldier throw up all over the floor, which was at least something interesting in an otherwise boring situation. I just sat there watching puke. There was a time when that would have grossed me out, but now I have seen it all.

1707 hrs

About all I did today was call home and have some lunch. It is really boring here. I can't imagine how bored I would have been if I had been stationed here in Kuwait for a year.

2019 hrs

I watched *Rambo II* in the MWR building. I can't wait to get out of here, even if it is back to Iraq. I am ready to surrender to the sleep monster for the evening now.

3 Feb 1300 hrs

This afternoon I found an equipment yard where to sit and suntan. While I was there, some foreign workers gave me tea and cigarettes. While I don't really like tea, and I certainly don't smoke, I took them up on their offer. My experiences with these people from other countries have been very positive. No matter how little these folks from India and other countries have, they are still very generous. It is amazing seeing how little they have, yet they still offer it to others. So, after I smoked two cigarettes, my lungs were in total revolt. I was hacking and coughing the whole time. Let that be a lesson to you: don't smoke; it is stupid!

1715 hrs

Let the inspection games begin! We had to dump our bags out in the road to make sure no one was smuggling home ocelots or mortar rounds. So we dumped all our stuff and we only received a cursory look from the customs officials. I mean, it was so silly, hundreds of bags dumped on the ground, and for what? Who cares if a soldier is smuggling something home? We are the good guys. I am still suffering from the smokes I had earlier.

2100 hrs

Nothing but briefings all evening about what we can't take home and the like. As a last resort, there were five amnesty boxes where you could dump illegal things before letting customs search you and your bags. I waited until everyone had gone through the line, then I went to the boxes and had some mixed drinks with the air force personnel running the checkpoint. Yeah right; they did tell me that they find all sorts of interesting things in the boxes after everyone leaves. I actually told some other soldiers that. They just looked at me in disbelief.

Throughout the last two days, there was one soldier, whom I had never seen before, who kept showing up right next to me. He is a chaplain's assistant, and is in my unit. He has helped me carry all of my broadcasting equipment from one place to another the whole trip so far. I have several huge boxes filled with gear. He has had to help me, because Birmingham is nowhere to be seen when it comes to work. Either that or she forgot all about helping me with this gear. My money is on forgetting, which has been her track record all along. Like Lieutenant O'Neil said, "Birmingham is going to get someone killed before the command wakes up and realizes something is wrong!"

2230 hrs

All evening we have been locked down in one way or another. Right now we are on buses going down the highway to the airport. We are in a convoy of big tour buses, like Greyhound drives. There have been more reports of attackers roaming the streets here in Kuwait, so I will be happy to get to the airport.

4 Feb 0100 hrs

The plane hasn't taken off yet, but I am at least in a seat. On top of that, I am in first class on an American Airlines Boeing 777. When we walked in the door, we all stepped on some lawn turf from California. One attendant was responsible for ensuring we would be stepping onto American soil. It was a very nice and appreciated gesture. It still hasn't really hit me that I am going home yet. Perhaps when we get to Germany I will feel different. We have about a dozen soldiers who acted as baggage loaders for our flight. When they got on the plane, we had to make room for them in first class and business class as well. I offered to give up my seat, no problem, when asked. Birmingham and Welch displayed little integrity and just sat there until it was determined that they weren't on the baggage detail. Because I had volunteered to give up my seat, I was allowed to keep it by the crew. The other two went to the back of the bus, so to speak.

0200 hrs

The plane is finally taking off; we will be flying right over Baghdad on our way to Germany. Just think, all the effort I went through to get to Kuwait from Baghdad, and now I will be flying right over it again. I'm going to try to take a little nap.

0330 hrs

Couldn't sleep. I had a nightmare about being on the ground in Iraq in the midst of the fighting. Now I am hanging out with the stewardesses. All of the American Airlines staff is being super friendly and nice to all of us. It is so nice to talk to people who have nothing to do with the war at all.

0400 hrs

Another time zone change just occurred, so although I have been flying for hours, it may not seem like that to you. I spent the entire time yapping with the flight attendants. One of them is involved in a program called "Angel Coin." In a nutshell, when a soldier is flown to Iraq, they are given a lead coin with an angel on it. When they return from Iraq, the crew asks if anyone still has their coin. One soldier on the flight, from my company, actually had his coin, which he had kept for the last twelve months. Sandy is the one who has spearheaded the effort. Although she works for American Airlines, this is a project of her own initiative. She gave me a coin on this flight, although I told her to save it for a soldier going to Iraq. She wouldn't hear of it.

0820 hrs

We are getting closer to North America now. The local time is for Greenland, which is where we are flying past. This crew is really great. The pilot let us come up into the cockpit and even sit in his seat. I'll leave it at that, as I don't want to get him in any trouble. I was even able to help pass out the food to the rest of the soldiers, which was very interesting. I will never be rude to the help on a plane ever again, now that I realize how much work it takes to take care of everyone.

I'm very tired, as I haven't slept very much in the last thirty-six hours at all. I have my DVD player going right now, but I simply can't sit still on an airplane to save my life.

The local time now is 0747 hrs

I am chasing the sun and I seem to be winning the race.

0745 hrs

Another time zone crossed into. We are flying over Canada as I am writing this down. The pilot just let me get on the intercom and say we are crossing into American airspace, over the city of Detroit. That got quite a cheer out of the people who were awake. I then said I was in control of the airplane and that we had enough fuel to get to Cancun and would not be going to America. Then they cheered even louder.

1104 hrs

We are descending into Dallas Fort Worth now, where we will change crews for the third and final time. I don't think we will be able to get out here at the airport, as it is a quick changeover. I have spent almost the entire flight up out of my seat doing one thing or another. I have been keeping busy so I wouldn't be alone with my thoughts. Now, as I get closer to home, those thoughts I have been trying to avoid are going to become my reality, and they will have to be dealt with.

1300 hrs

This is the day that never ends. According to the flight information screen, we are four minutes from landing at Robert Gray Army Airfield in Fort Hood, Texas. This entire experience has changed me in ways that I have mentioned previously. I have tried to be as honest as I could in terms of things that happened while in Iraq. Obviously, due to security concerns, there were some things that will remain forever in my mind. Remember the prison abuse trials? There are some things better left unexposed to the public for many reasons. The plane will land and I, along with my fellow soldiers, will be combat veterans, something I always wanted to become. Writing this book has been very helpful to me in terms of identifying and dealing with my feelings. I hope I don't appear different to my friends and family over the coming months.

Final approach. Raise a glass of non-water to those who didn't come home, to the rest of my life, and perhaps even to peace in our time.

Wheels down, tires squealing.

The End.

Epilogue:

I am home now and happy to be here. I won't include many of the details, because they don't apply to what I went through in Iraq. I have drawn several conclusions, though, that I will share with you now. We are winning the "War on Terror." I can say this because of my personal observations coupled with worldwide events. As for my enemies in the country of Iraq, it was not the terrorists that I had to worry about; it was my very own coworkers and superiors. This observation was made by a friend of mine who happened to read this before it ever became a book. These people did everything in their power to restrict any sort of positive thing I had going. After talking to my wife about it, she thinks we should move to Europe, because I get along with them so much better than my American peers.

Lastly, I am very glad that I took the time to write these things down, not only because you may chose to read it, but because it helped me as well. I would gladly have stayed longer in Iraq if the army had let me. I will go back again if told, but would rather have stayed if it meant I wouldn't have to return later. As I have said over and over, "Staying is easy, leaving is hard."